Race Matters
in Pain Medicine

HOW I MADE MONEY, LOST 90 LBS.,
AND THRIVED IN CHRONIC PAIN

Written by Jackson Dunbar, Esq.

Illustrations by Chanel Samone

D1073504

Copyright © 2022 Jackson Dunbar, Esq.

A Jackson Dunbar Origin Story

All rights reserved. This book or any portion thereof may not be reproduced or used in any manner whatsoever without the express written permission of the publisher except for the use of brief quotations in a book review.

This publication is designed to provide accurate and authoritative information about the subject matter covered. It is sold with the understanding that the Author is not engaged in rendering legal, medical, accounting or other professional service. If expert advice is required, the service of a competent professional person should be sought.

Library of Congress Cataloging -in-Publication Data

Race Matters in Pain Medicine:

How I Made Money, Lost 90lbs. and Thrive in Chronic Pain.

ISBN: 979-8-218-01815-3; 979-8-218-01816-0

INTRODUCTION

Race Matters in Pain Medicine! As a result, we are left with the critical under-medication of African Americans, who suffer with unbearable Chronic Pain and the severe over-medication of White Americans, which helped cause the Opioid Crisis.

My name is Jackson Dunbar, Esq. I am a father, husband, entrepreneur and suffer from Chronic Pain. As a Chronic Pain patient, I sought "soup to nuts" solutions that could help manage pain, improve quality of life, and provide for my family. Medical experts did help, but their reliance on purely evidence-based Western Medicine favored solutions that were purely medicinal and/or surgical, nothing more. Those "solutions' barely got me off the couch and did nothing to help provide for my family as I was unable to work. Thus, I was on my own to develop methods to make money for my family, lose weight and thrive while being in Chronic Pain.

To be clear, I am not a medical expert, so obtain the approval of your own providers before adopting the solutions in this book. I possess advanced degrees in Law (Juris Doctor) and Business (Master of Business Administration), spending much of my 25-year career developing innovative solutions that help Fortune 500 companies and myself make money. This type of Ideation was extremely useful in my life as a serial Entrepreneur, granting me the ability to:

- Find Opportunity.
- Develop the opportunity into a job-creating businesses.

- Turn those businesses into profit generators that help improve my local community.

This type of "business logic" requires problem-solving that creates specific solutions to keep people employed at a reasonable profit. I've used "business logic" my entire 25+ year business career and soon discovered that this thought process could be applied to my health recovery. Stated another way, I applied "business logic" to solve the problem of my Chronic Pain.

First, any problem can be solved **IF** you have the "right" team assembled to craft a solution. This was true in "Business" and in "Health"; as I spent a small fortune finding the "right" experts in Modern and Alternative Medicine to help me solve the "problem" of my Chronic Pain.

It took years of "kissing frogs" to build a "Wellness" Team tasked with helping me create a "process" to improve my quality of life. **The result** was this book, which includes all the methods I used to **Make Money, Lose 90lbs and Thrive while in Chronic Pain.** This book is "Soup to Nuts," which means it will take you from the origins of my pain to dealing with insurance companies, selecting lawyers and doctors to live a life where you Thrive in Chronic Pain.

Chronic Pain Patients and Caregivers should read this book, so both parties have parity of information and know what to expect. Then after receiving approval from your doctor, apply the methods as appropriate so you can Make Money, Lose Weight and Thrive in Chronic Pain.

Medical Professionals should use this book as both a resource for their patients who seek a holistic solution for their pain and quality of life; and as "Bias Training" to prevent inaccurate diagnosis and treatment of pain patients.

Behavioral Health Professionals should use this book for patients with Anxiety and Depression diagnosis due to Chronic Pain, as our methods promote sustained mental health.

Parents seeking a tool to educate themselves and their children on the impact of institutional racism in Pain Medicine should read this book for two reasons:
- To ensure the viability of current pain treatment plans.
- Learn **"positive tactics"** to overcome Institutional Racism.

Individuals seeking to start a discussion on Inequities in the Medical System and how it negatively impacts society should not only read this book but do something to make things better. I do not care if you are Black, White or Polka dot; if you suffer from Chronic Pain, then you are my "***Brothers and Sisters in Pain***". Our shared loss was largely "mishandled by the government whose overreaching guidelines did more to punish than heal. Further, costly medical procedures promised a "cure"; often failed to get the job done, left us isolated with no hope of success. We have a right to be "Angry"! This book will teach you how to use that emotion to improve your quality of life.

In closing, I recruited the right "Wellness" experts who helped me Make Money, Lose 90lbs, and Thrive In Chronic Pain. I put those "**Methods**" into this "solutions-based" book and pray you find it of use on your Chronic Pain journey.

Be blessed,
Jackson Dunbar, Esq.

ABOUT THE AUTHOR

Jackson Dunbar, Esq. is the Founder of WellMed/Atlanta and a Social Entrepreneur and Philanthropist that seeks to build profitable companies that produce socially responsible products and services.

Mr. Dunbar is proud of his "Blue Collar" roots. The son of a Custodian and Seamstress, Mr. Dunbar was the first man in his family to graduate from college – Stockton University. He would later receive a Juris Doctor from the Tulane University School of Law and an MBA from the Thunderbird School of Global Management.

A true son of the 'South", Mr. Dunbar can trace his Entrepreneurship "roots" back to the 1940s when his Great Grand Father, Jackson "Jack" Dunbar, built the Dunbar Hotel – the largest Black-Owned Hotel in Florida. Also, Mr. Dunbar's father -- the son of a Sharecropper -- taught his children to ***Work Hard, Manage Money Well, and Never Give Up!***

With this philosophy in mind, Mr. Dunbar started a landscaping and snow removal business at the "ripe" old age of thirteen to help with family expenses after his parents' divorce. "I saw my mother crying in front of an empty refrigerator one night after we moved to New Jersey and swore to become her "financial" blessing one day." Years later, Mr. Dunbar would "retire" his mother early and move her into a dream home in sunny Florida.

He would spend years in Corporate America working in the fields of Product Ideation, Product Development, Market Analysis, and Product Development before saving the initial capital to open WellMed/Atlanta – A Group of Child & Adolescent Psychiatrists serving Metro Atlanta.

As the Concept originator of the Mobile Psychiatric Services platform that developed into WellMed/Atlanta, Mr. Dunbar was responsible for all B2C/B2B direct marketing, business development and grew the staff from a solo practitioner in 2007 to one of the largest Black-Owned Psychiatric Consulting Firms in Metro Atlanta by 2014. In 2015, due to its strong double digit growth rates during the "Great Recession," WellMed/Atlanta was one of only twenty businesses in the state of Georgia selected by the SBA for its Emerging Leaders Program.

Mr. Dunbar and his son would be involved in a car accident caused by a distracted driver. By the miracle of God, his son Miles was playing soccer just two days later. Mr. Dunbar would need dozens of back procedures; and, in the end, found himself in constant pain for the rest of his days. He also requires a scooter and pain medications that causes significant cognitive impairment.

As a Disabled American, Mr. Dunbar spends his days in rehab, swimming, and being a Servant Leader in his local community. By "marshaling" the Time, Talent, and Treasure of himself and volunteers, Mr. Dunbar offers Teacher Bonuses, Computer Equipment, and Mental Health & Financial Literacy Education to schools in his locality. He states, "I have good and bad days but chose to focus on the light in front of me instead of the darkness behind."

Mr. Dunbar has been married for almost 20 years to his wife Monique and has two children – Miles and Becky. His family lives in Tucker, Georgia – a small city about ten miles from Atlanta. He speaks Spanish and German, having lived and studied in Guadalajara, Jalisco, Mexico, and Cologne "Koln," Germany. Mr. Dunbar's hobbies include Cooking, "Cane-Martial Arts," and Swimming.

Dedication

I wanted to thank my wife for remaining by my side – good times and bad. To my kids, thank you for being my source of strength in my time of strife.

Thank you, Mom, for all your sacrifices and for being the strongest person I've ever known. Thank you, Dad, for teaching me to *"Word Hard, Manage Money Well and Never Give Up"*!

Thank you, Grandmom, for gifting me the love of books and a desire to travel the world.

To my "**Thrive Team**":

- **Howard** - You are the type of friend that comes along once in a lifetime. Thank you for your wisdom and for being there no matter the storm or saving grace. You continue to be a blessing to me and my family.

- *Lorna* - From the ***Wade Walker YMCA*** -- you gave me a safe place to "rehab" my broken body every day.

- *Linda* - Thank you for not giving up on me. You helped me "transition" into an "Enabled Life" where a "scooter" becomes my "tool" for independence.

- *Beth* - From the ***Decatur/Dekalb YMCA*** – you taught me to swim without the use of my legs; and in doing so, gave me an escape from my Chronic Pain.

- *Vicki* - You taught me that anything strength/toning exercise that could be completed in a gym, could be done in a pool. Your Aquatic Training keeps my "core" strong, and my pain manage.

- ***GrandMaster Robaina*** - You helped me change my Disability into Advantage! Your inspired teachings and ***never quit attitude*** are a gifted tool to help manage my physical and mental health.

- ***Rory and Jeff*** - From the **Stone Mountain Public House**, you gave me a comfortable place where I could eat great food, smoke a cigar and listen to smooth Jazz while writing this book.

Thank you all for getting me through the bad times and strengthening my resolve to live a purpose driven life.

To my Illustrator, thank you for doing all the revisions with a smile and for always delivering beyond expectations.

Thank you to my Ancestors who farmed this land, built this great country for no money, and died in its defense while being treated as second-class citizens. Know that I am here because of your noble sacrifices.

Lastly, I wanted to thank my lifelong friend Thomas Laigaie "Father Tommy" who died far too soon from a Covid-induced heart attack. Know that proceeds from this book will go to support your mission to heal the sick, shelter the homeless, and feed the hungry. To learn more about "Father Tommy's mission, scan the below QR Code and/or visit – http://www.wellmedatlanta.threadless.com

Table of Contents

Chapter 1

For human beings to expect perfection in their lives is common. We think that's our only pursuit in life, to be successful and live a fulfilling life without any worries. It seldom happens, and just when we think that our life has picked up the right pace, some unfortunate hurdle spins it around, and before you even know it, you're off track within seconds.

It was a nice sunny day on February 5, 2015. My eight-year-old son, Miles, played soccer for a local team that practiced near Downtown Decatur. I left my daughter with my wife, drove down Brockett Rd, and saw there was a lot of traffic on I78. Turning around, I decided to drive down E Ponce de Leon Rd to get to Decatur. I knew this was the longer route, but there would be no traffic on this back road. I knew this because our church is located on E Ponce de Leon, and so we have driven on this road for years both for Sunday worship and after-work church volunteer activities during the week.

I thought of the mid-six-figure deal I just closed for our small company – WellMed/Atlanta: A company my wife and I started in 2007. A group of Board-Certified Psychiatrists offering mental health services to families and individuals, as well as Psychiatric Consulting services to businesses and schools. It was my best idea and has become a lucrative business, that gives back to its local community.

My wife, a graduate of Emory Medical School, and myself, a local entrepreneur with advanced degrees in Law from Tulane University School of Law and Business from Thunderbird Graduate School of International Business, turned an idea into one of the largest private Minority-Owned Psychiatry consulting firms in our area – and we were just getting started!

I've closed big deals before during my Legal and Business Career, but that occurred while working for someone else. This Psychiatric Consulting deal's 35% profit margin would go into our pockets and become the seed money needed for our continued expansion.

My son was in the back of the car as we approached the corner of East Ponce de Leon and Interstate 285. He asked me if we were still going biking around Stone Mountain on Saturday. Miles loved to race me on our bikes. I used to bike him around Stone Mountain when he was younger to train for Sprint Triathlons.

We also liked renting bikes and exploring when visiting other countries. It was a very good excuse for spending time with family. I told him we would do it after his soccer game. He said that would not be fair because he would be too tired to keep up. I told him that I would carry his five-year-old sister Becky in the bike stroller to make it even.

Miles said, "deal," as I had the green light and continued to drive straight. Suddenly, this car failed to yield and turned right into us. We collided! My car went into a big curb. My airbags deployed, and I tasted something funny in the air. I yelled to my son and asked if he was okay. He said yes, cried that his stomach hurt, and asked me if the car was going to explode.

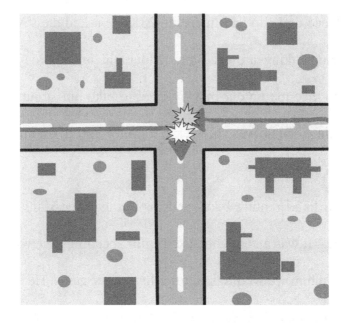

I asked Miles to get out of the car and remembered we had the child locks on. I got out of the car and opened his car door, gave him a big hug while checking to ensure he was free of injury, thanking God that Miles was not killed. I told him to come with me, and we went over to the driver to make sure she was ok.

She came out of her car and apologized for causing the accident. She thought I was turning right onto I285. I asked her if she saw my turning lights on. The driver didn't, "but many people don't use their signals in Atlanta," she then stated. We then called the Police, and it took them about an hour to show. During that time, I made sure both she and my son stayed calm, then went and looked at my car. I believed she said this was her second accident in a month.

My car was a 2004 BMW 525i. It was my father's car. My father was a Blue-Collar Man. He is a Vietnam Veteran who served his nation honorably. He also had a great work ethic, often working a side "Hustle" job in addition to his normal eight hours job. Both of my parents worked to make sure their children got a good education, and I was doing the same.

My dad loved cars but never had the money to buy a nice one. While attending my wedding in late 2003, he showed me a picture of his new car, the 2004 BMW 525i. He really babied that car, only driving it on Saturdays, washing it every weekend, and keeping it in a garage with a carpeted floor. He only had about 5000 miles on the car when he discovered that he had Leukemia in 2009.

My dad was tough; he was a strong man. He would live another seven months, despite the doctors only giving him two weeks to live. He gave me the car. My wife and I were starting our business, and my dad told me I needed a "made for success" car when going on sales calls. It is funny; I felt my dad was with me every time I drove to close a deal. He would say, "***Work Hard, Be Tight with Money and Never Give Up***!"

I thought about all of that as I saw his car, which, by the looks of it, was going to be totaled. Don't get me wrong, I am beyond happy that everyone was able to walk away from the accident unscathed, but I lost my connection to him that day. My heart broke when I saw that car's fate; it wasn't a bearable sight. I wondered if I could get it fixed, but that would really be a stretch.

I tried to comfort the young woman that we were fine while I held my son as tight as I could. Five cars stopped and asked the young lady if she was fine or needed help. Miles asked why they were asking her for help since she had caused the accident. It was odd, even to a kid.

Miles was seven years old, and I had never had "***THE TALK***" with him. The **"talk"** every Black man must have with his kids about Race in America. I told him that those White drivers assumed I was at fault because I was Black, and they had an impulse to pro-tect the White Woman that drove the other car.

It was then that I realized it was time to tell him about racial dis-crimination. I told him about how Black People, too often, are not treated as well as White people in this country that was built by

African Americans and protected during times of war by five generations of Black Men and Women – our ancestors.

I told my children that we must work twice as hard and be twice as good at anything we do to get half as far as White people in this country. I always taught them to work hard regardless of the hurdles. After all, it was the hard work and work ethic of his mother and I, owing to which we were the first man and woman in our family to graduate from college. It was also the secret "sauce" to running our successful business.

We told the officer what happened, and the driver stated she was at fault. The officer reviewed the scene, both cars, and then gave the driver a ticket. During that time, my wife and the defendant's boyfriend came to the scene. I told the gentleman to take the defendant home as she was shaken. My wife asked me how I was doing; I told her my wrist and groin hurt and felt a pain in my lower back. She told me to go to the emergency room, and that would be the first of many medical appointments to come.

I would then begin treatment at Emory Back and Spine for the next seven years. They had a fine facility, and it seemed like they listened to me about my pain. I had groin, lower back pain, and nerve pain that I felt in my leg and left foot. I was diagnosed with a Herniated Disk, for which they gave me a back brace and started to treat my back pain gently.

I think back to that day; it had a great start, but I ended up with an injury that would make all my coming months a living hell. For six or seven months after the accident, I was doing rehab, and they put me on pain medicine. It was too much to bear; I was in constant pain, and there was no stop to it. I can't say I ever got used to the pain. The pain medicine that I was on made me gain a lot of weight. My movements were hindered due to the pain, and so was my productivity.

I was still the same man; only the pain was so bad that it occupied a lot of my headspace. It elevated to the point I couldn't even walk.

Of course, the treatments were ongoing, but the doctors straight up refused to operate on me because my blood pressure was constantly very high. Every time we checked, it would be 190/120 or worse, and the doctors just couldn't operate on me with that blood pressure. It was crazy! In fact, all my numbers were red. I was basically in the danger zone, and my body was not cooperating at all.

Then the fallout occurred. It was when my weight reached 300 pounds. A major part of the problem was the medications I was being given for pain management. I believe my numbers wouldn't be this way if it wasn't for the medication. Everything worked against me because the medicines were important for my pain apparently, but they also caused all that weight gain. And in turn, the weight gain increased the pain even more. So, for several months, I was in this constant loop of pain, and there was nothing the doctors did to make it better.

Chapter 2

There are many aspects to life and to the things that happen to us. One event can have a significant impact on more than one thing in our lives. The trick is to stay vigilant and keep an eye out for yourself. And in times when we can't, our loved ones do it for us.

My mother always believed that Insurance Companies were the biggest **"Pyramid Schemes"** to exist on the planet. I realized that her word had substance and what she believed was 100% true.

The thing is that you can't just get out of these situations without a mess. On the one hand, I had an evident injury. On the other, my insurance company, "Snake 1," and the Driver's "Snake 2" called and wanted to investigate me about the accident. As a lawyer, I knew that this would be the start of a long process to ensure that my car, medical bills, and pain were fairly compensated.

My wife Monique was concerned about me having to tend to so many other issues while being in pain. She said, "You can't talk to them while you are medicated as your senses will be dulled." As one of the foremost Child and Adolescent Psychiatrists in the state, Monique was on point, as the medicine gave me "Pill Brain." In other words, I felt either high or sleepy all the time, which meant I would be easy pickings for the well-trained insurance adjusters and would be more susceptible to their "nickel and diming"

tactics. The only issue with going off meds was that I would be in immense pain, which meant mentally incapacitated; thus, easy pickings for the insurance "vultures".

I thought about it as a lawyer and developed a process for answering Insurance Adjusters' Questions while being medicated:

- I would come off the medications and schedule talks with the insurance adjusters early morning. This allowed me to be more attentive as I would not be in as much pain as the day had just started.

- Write a scripted statement about what happened, complete with questions the insurance company might ask, so I would not be surprised by the adjusters.

- Have my staff ask me questions about the accident, answering only with the answers to my scripted statement. This practice would train me to either answer with a scripted response or say "I do not recall" during the depositions.

As luck would turn out, I only had to leave recorded statements with both insurance companies. "Snake 2", the driver's insurer, totaled my car and offered only 75% of the car's total market value as payment for auto damages. I told the S.O.B to "Lawyer Up" because I would do so as they were really giving me a hard time.

Then I called "Snake 1," my insurer; they offered 112% of my car's value minus my 500 deductibles. I accepted their offer and then looked for a lawyer in anticipation of a fight with "Snake 2" to fairly compensate me for pain and medical expenses; I was not going down without a fight.

The driver of the other car accepted responsibility for her actions. She was a White woman, about 5'7" tall, and had Cobb County tags – a predominately White area of town. As I was a Black Man, suing this person meant I would be at a disadvantage because the criminal justice system was designed to protect White Women and Men. This meant I needed a White lawyer in case this went to a jury, as the majority of the jurors would be White. I was given the names of three Lawyers: Two Females and One Male; all had a strong connection in Cobb County. I interviewed the two women.

They were very sharp, but the bulk of their practice was Family Law.

The next thing I did was to visit the Law Firm **"We Win No Excuses, LLC."** and meet Peter Parker. This man looked like Captain America: Tall, Blond, and well-built! This guy had some personality. We just stared at each other, sizing one another like two boxers in a ring. He knew how to dress for a client interview: No power suit, just dockers and a custom polo shirt; however, he wore a Tag Heuer Carrera Heritage Watch – which had to cost over $5,000. He had over 20 years of Personal Injury Trial experience, and his firm had over 10 locations across the South.

I was thoroughly impressed by this man's profile and understood that he was competent enough to handle my case. After sharing the details regarding my case, I knew I had found my lawyer just by his responses. He came off as a trustworthy person; he was attractive and had a southern "twang" to his speech that the jury pool in Cobb County would love.

We spoke for several hours, after which Peter agreed to take me on as a client. He said, "I'll get you the maximum judgment permitted by law." Peter was a man of his words, and he won my trust right away, and I think I did the same.

"Jackson," he stated, "I love clients like you."

To be fair, he made some very good points about my case and gave me a lot of hope. Here are a few things Peter told me that made a lot of sense:

- The other driver was clearly at fault, which was admitted in her own statement and the Police summary, so that was evidence.

- You, as a lawyer and business owner, are well-spoken, clean-cut, with a family, possessing strong roots in the community.

- Your business also helps the community, so you won't be seen as an opportunist if this goes to trial.

"Snake 2" will "cave" and pay the policy limits associated with the driver's compensation, the driver's Policy. The real fight would be with "Snake 1" because your injuries will be much higher than what Allstate is obligated to pay. At that point, "Snake 1" must "step up" and cover your medical bills, and "Snake 1," as they have been called, has the best legal defense team on the planet! Peter then shook my hand and told me to concentrate on getting well and let him fight with " ." I was happy to do so as I had handed over my case to a very capable lawyer. Besides, I had to look after my health and the never-ending pain.

After the incident, I had countless visits to the hospital. The treatment was ongoing, and so was the pain. For whatever reason, it didn't seem to go away. I knew I needed to take more steps if I were to get rid of this pain. I inspected the Emory Physical Therapy and loved the facility. In my first few visits, I made it very clear to the team that I did not want surgery. I was determined to do whatever it took to work myself back to health.

Consequently, I was given stronger medications and put on a kick-ass physical therapy plan. I was more than happy with it, if there was no surgery involved. I would go to therapy and do the exercises at home that the therapist would tell me. I took them very seriously as I knew this was the only way for improvement.

As for the medications, I had to get used to them as well. I hated sitting at work. My back hurt like hell, especially if I twisted while sitting down. It was getting impossible with every passing day. I would bark at my employees for making small mistakes and come down on Corporate Clients who were only one day late with their payments. I was way out of line during that time. Of course, I reflected on my behavior, but I couldn't do much about it. The pain kept aggravating so much that we had to keep a bag of frozen peas in our office fridge to help cool down the pain, which calmed the nerves far better than any cold pack I've ever used.

I tend to walk fast naturally, which created a jarring impact that hurt my back even more. The use of a cane slowed me down and took some pressure off my back. I got another injection which gave me the hiccups, but I did not get the type of relief I received from the first injection.

It was also tough learning how to manage the medications. I would be in a constant state of pain without them, but grogging and off my game when I took them. During negotiation, I once made a mistake by giving away too much without getting enough in return. Clearly, it impacted my performance. I needed to find a way to work while I was on medication. So, I scheduled more appointments by teleconference and fixed important negotiations during a time when my pain was better managed.

As for my personal life, it was affected too. Spring Break was ahead of us, and my wife wanted to see her family residing in Washington DC. Although I was completing stronger exercises in Rehab during that time, I was no way near strong enough to deal with an 11-hour drive to that town. Nor did I have the strength for a "walking vacation" through DC.

I knew it broke my wife's heart when I told her this. She did not speak to me for the rest of the night. Monique, my wife, is a good woman who worked hard to build our home. She more than deserved that trip, and I hated breaking her heart this way, but things were not in my favor.

The next day, she came back and suggested taking a family cruise. It was ½ the drive time to Orlando, and the ship had plenty of services and excursions for people with mobility needs. As I said, my wife is a good woman, and she knows how to take things forward. She had a real problem-solving mind and looked at things very practically.

Chapter 3

I have learned that whatever you do in life, do it with utmost

dedication and honesty. If you really want to realize your

dreams, you must work hard for them; there is no exception!

There was a lot of chaos in my life during that time, but we were soon met with a very good news. Our small business – WellMed/Atlanta – was selected to participate in the SBA's Emerging Leaders Program. Each year, the SBA selected 20 small businesses in 20 different states to participate in an incubator-type program designed to help small businesses get to the next level. It had a highly competitive selection process, and we barely made the revenue threshold, but the selection committee liked us because:

- We had consistent revenue growth rates since 2009.
- We were committed to our social responsibility.
- Sought to create local jobs.
- Lastly, the selection supervisor liked my work ethic. My interview occurred about six weeks after the accident, and I was in serious pain. I think she saw that, but I still finished the three-hour interview, and that was the difference-maker.

The program would help us develop a three (3) to five (5) year strategic growth plan to take our business to the next level. We would be broken into small groups of five, and a group of consultants would examine our growth plans.

I was so proud that we were selected. WellMed/Atlanta was little more than a concept written on a napkin in 2008. Monique and I had to sacrifice a lot to realize that dream, giving up good-paying jobs, living below our means, and eating beans and rice often when our friends were going out. In fact, we would often joke that many of our patients dressed better than us. Now, God was finally going to reward our business stewardship by granting us the knowledge to expand our small business, perform our social responsibility, create more jobs, and possibly achieve the American Dream together as husband and wife.

After the initial processes were complete, I finally met with my SBA group. It was a small one, but these successful business owners were sharp and wealthy. They came from different fields and had expertise in different industries. After our first interaction, I knew we would learn a lot from each other as I was ready to share my wisdom with them.

As our first task, we were asked to share each other's financials and solve business questions that kept each of us from growing. I was a little embarrassed. Not only did all these people generate at least twice as much revenue as us, but their margins were also higher as well. One of my colleagues joked, "WellMed/Atlanta just squeaked into this program by the hair of its skinny chin."

I made it clear to them that WellMed/Atlanta was a psychiatric medical practice that also functioned as a psychiatric medical consulting firm. I said, *"Our goal is to provide superior mental health services, for example, our patient sessions are twice as long as our competitors to ensure outstanding care.*

Whether you have a child with ADHD or a spouse with depression, we are always there to provide our services. Yes, this means we make less money, but we want to make sure that every one of our patients has the tools they need to succeed in the real world."

At that time, my group then laughed at our firm's social mandate. Later, they discovered my business and marketing analytical acumen was useful in helping solve the key business questions they had with their companies. "All those years crunching data in Corporate America was useful after all," I joked.

It was a good day in terms of learning; I even identified weaknesses in my strategies that I was ignoring all along. I couldn't wait to go home and tell Monique all about the meeting. I told her how cooperative all of them were, as I had informed them about my injury, and they were cool about my need for meeting time flexibility due to my medication schedule. I think it went fine, but it was a milestone for Monique and me in our WellMed/Atlanta journey.

While my professional life was going on its track, I made sure not to neglect my pain. My health remained my priority all through those years. I was putting in a lot of effort at the rehab but still thought I was hitting a wall at some point. PT, my provider, seemed to be very good at her job. We were on stretching, twisting, and strength-building exercises. She was successful in taking me up to the point of pain and then cooling things down, so I did not hurt myself.

We were slowly building up our pace, as well as my pain tolerance. The best part of the treatment was the end of the sessions when she would put electrodes on me and shoot me with electricity. I would lay on an ice pad during all that time, and it felt great. It was easy to talk to her, and we would only go as far as I could handle. I understood that my pain management was going to take long enough for the pain to entirely go away. I couldn't wait to fully recover as that would negatively impact my personal life.

When my wife asked me about the vacation, I saw how happy she was, so eventually, I agreed to it. I thought I could use that quality family time too, and we all could unwind from all the inconvenience we were put through, especially with insurance.

We had our vacation on a Royal Caribbean cruise, and I felt like I had let my family down. The ship was beautiful, and we brought my mother so she could help with the kids. Two days into the cruise, all my medications were "thrown" away by the person who cleaned our cabin. The idiot thought the medications were trash, and so he dumped them without even asking. It honestly sounded like a bad excuse, as my wife informed me that some of the drugs had street value. She believed that the medications were stolen under the pretense of being thrown away.

Of course, we went ahead and complained to the managers on the ship, who apologized right away, but I was screwed because I was out of medication in the middle of the sea! They immediately sent me to their ship Physician. This guy was nothing like the ship doctor on the Love Boat. He and his entire staff were rude and abrasive. We told him what had happened, and he did not believe us.

He treated me like I was a drug-seeking perp and said they could only give me Excedrin for the pain. Consequently, the rest of the trip was a painful experience. I told Monique she could take the kids on the excursions without me. Thank God my mother was there, as she was able to pick up my slack. The whole thing just felt very depressing, as I could not pull my weight. I never thought about locking up my medication during a vacation; this was a lesson learned the hard way!

After getting back, one fine day, I was doing my laundry when my whole leg went numb, and I fell to the ground. I knew right away that something was wrong; I was in immense pain, and my son ran upstairs and found me that way. I was so embarrassed! I lied, told him I was fine, and crawled to the bed, praying he did not worry. I don't know why but it seemed as if the pain was getting worse. I can't remember how many steroid injections I had, but they didn't seem to work anymore. They took the edge off for a bit but then wore off quickly. I did not want surgery, but the pain was so bad! On top of that, the side effects from the medication made me feel like I was losing my mind.

The Emory MD stated that further injections would be a waste of time and that I should consider surgery. He offered me a surgery consultant, and I gladly accepted it. Just the same, I got a second opinion at Sports Medicine South, where the head physician was a former professional soccer player. He then decided to execute his plan B career – becoming an Orthopedic Surgeon.

I talked to the Sports Medicine "guy," and told him about my condition, and he wanted to do an Electromyography (**EMG**), a test designed to detect neuromuscular abnormalities. They wanted me to take the procedure, no meds, no food, no coffee; this was going to suck. And I was right to think that way; it was extremely painful and sucked!

They hooked me up to these wires, which was not so bad initially. The painful part was when I had to twist my body as they shot me with electricity. Twisting was awfully painful. I still remember the trauma from that procedure, and for this reason, I am always careful getting out of bed, sitting in a car, or even using the toilet.

The procedure went on for over an hour. It required me to twist in a painful position, then hold it as they shot me with electricity. It was something I would never want to repeat. By the end, I was informed that the herniated disk had caused permanent nerve damage, and to fix that, surgery was a necessity, something that I dreaded.

Chapter 4

If there is one skill required the most in this world, it is the ability to bounce back. As humans, I think resilience is what keeps us going. It is a beautiful word but very difficult to abide by.

I tried everything I could to avoid surgery. Heaven knows it was the last option that I never wanted to resort to. But it looked like I didn't have many options left. The first one I met was Dr. Ortho, an Orthopedic Surgeon at Emory. She looked tough and the kind of person who's good at their job. She was about 5'3" with a New York accent and grit that fit her swag. Her team told me that my surgery would occur right before Thanksgiving. I told them I did not want surgery at the beginning of this process, but now, I was willing to do whatever it took to stop the pain.

They wanted to do a Laminectomy. It seemed like the best option to stop my pain. Monique did not like the idea of surgery, but she hated seeing me in pain. It was a slippery slope. I didn't want to spend any more time in pain than I already did. Of course, it was not just taking a toll on me but also on those that were close to me.

Once, I caught her crying during the whole deal. I realized that so much had been put on her since the accident. I had to really get it back under control so I could go on doing regular duties. Anyway, the decision was made. It was difficult, but it needed to be done. Dr. Ortho's team told me that the pre-surgery consult would occur the day before the surgery, and we would go from there.

I had so much to do before the surgery. We worked for ourselves, so there was so much work from the office I had to complete before I went in for it, as I would probably be out of the office for the remainder of the year as I needed the time to recover.

Near the date of the surgery, I also had my SBA Emerging Leaders Strategic Growth Presentation and Graduation. I thought I timed my medication to coincide with my presentation, but we went two hours over. By the time I presented, not only was I in pain, but I also had the "Pill Brain." I got through the presentation somehow but was not at the top of my game. Our professor stated he loved our strategic growth plan and introduced me to several Financiers who attended. I told him that as soon as my surgery was over, we would "pull the trigger on the plan" and thanked him for his guidance and support during the program.

The graduation went by smoothly as well. Ceasar Mitchell, the President of the Atlanta City Council, officiated, and it gave Monique and me an opportunity to network and start relationships with some Atlanta city officials. It wasn't easy to go through it, especially since I was in so much pain. I just wished my father was alive to see this day. He would have been proud of our ability to turn an idea into a service that was recognized by city officials for the public good that it does.

I had Pre-Op, and it was terrible. I went off medication thinking I would only be there for a couple of hours. Dr. Ortho and her team saw me and stated that they might have to cut more of me because of my weight. Turned out that I had gained a lot of weight since the accident because of the medication, and I weighed about 350lbs, which could obviously be a problem during the operation. The medical team wanted me to know that the operation might be a bit more evasive. Then, Dr. Ortho wanted another MRI because she could not see the original MRI I had taken back in March 2015. Of course, I had to go inside the MRI machine that was small and climbing into the machine aggravated my lower back and nerve pain. It was so bad that I had begun to sweat.

I picked up my mother from the airport as she had planned on staying with us for the rest of the year. We had our Office Christmas Party, and I just completed the Ethnic Marketing Initiative for my church. A lot of work went into that plan, and I did it for free. My Pastor asked me to present my findings to our Vestry – Church Elders. As I drove to the church, I passed the spot where the accident had occurred. It triggered a painful memory in my head, but I continued driving to church and received a call from Emory. It was a nurse stating that my surgery had been canceled. I demanded to know why, and she stated that Dr. Ortho would call me the next day and explain everything.

I sat in the church parking lot. I was very angry, and my body was shaking. I wondered what I was going to do? I was in so much pain and was tired of feeling this way. I sat there stranded in my car, and I had to go before my Pastor and Church Elders to present the findings. I was a mess at that time; I still don't know how I gathered the courage to present.

I prayed for strength and thought about my father. I repeated his motto, "***Work Hard, Be Tight With Money, and Never Give Up!***" I picked myself up, put my game face on, and repeated my father's words repeatedly. That day, I gave one of the best presentations I've ever given. The Q&A session was tough as I was in pain, and it was tough to manage my emotions, but I knew I could succeed.

Once I was done, my Pastor met me and told stated I did a good job with the presentation. I thanked him as I really needed his appreciation at that time. Then I told him my surgery was canceled right before the presentation and that it had me worried.

The next day, I drove my mother to take Miles and Becky to school. Once we dropped them off, I received a call from Dr. Ortho. I asked her what the issue was, and she stated my numbers were --

TOTAL SHIT:

- My blood pressure was inside the stroke range

- Weight was around 350lbs

- AIC was 8.7

- All my other vitals were in the red

Me @ 350lbs

I understood that it was dangerous, but I told her that she had to do the surgery. She had no idea how much pain I deal with every day, and I practically wanted to get rid of it as soon as I could. I told her that I had to pay neighborhood kids to help train my son for soccer, that I was burdening my wife by not being able to pull my own weight, and that I was tired of being in a constant state of agony. I begged her to do the surgery.

PAIN-ENDING SURGERY

She stated it was my own fault and that I should have taken better care of myself over the years. Before the accident, I rarely used my medical benefits. In fact, I could not figure out why my rates kept going up even though I had not completed a medical exam in years. I then asked her what the next steps were, and she said she would put me in touch with Emory Primary Care, and they would try to improve my numbers.

I went home in that state and asked my mother and wife what I was going to do. I'm glad I had their support through it all. We prayed together, and my wife agreed with Dr. Ortho. Monique reviewed my numbers and said that I would have stroked out had Emory operated on me and that I should listen to whatever Primary Care said.

I met Dr. PCP a couple of days later. He was in his 70's, and we had a lot in common. We both used to box and play the piano. We talked about our kids and families before the examination began. He was the only White doctor to ever lay hands on me during an examination. Dr. PCP was a former paratrooper and an Army doctor, so his examination was up close and personal to ascertain the extent of my injury. I called it a "**ME TOO**" exam as I was butt naked as he essentially examined me "everywhere." This was one of the most thorough medical exams that I've ever had. But I appreciated Dr. PCP's concern and his seriousness toward my case. This man was nothing like the doctor I meant on the Royal Caribbean cruise.

When finished, he looked at me and asked if I wanted to die? I told him I didn't and that I had a family. The next thing he told me was to lose weight. Now, the next big question was, how? How could I shed all that weight when I could barely be active with all that pain? Had I been healthy, I could drop the weight easily by just training in the gym. In fact, I never would've allowed this to happen. Right now, I need a robust plan in place to get into shape.

Dr. PCP sat across me; we looked at each other briefly before he asked me if I could swim? He told me to go swimming using the Breaststroke and to cut calories to 1800 per day. He then put me on medications to help control my B/P and A1C. Dr. PCP then looked me in the eye and said, "You are going to listen to me!" This guy was an **Old School Gangster** with an MD. He had so much vigor in his voice. I instantly agreed and was then committed to doing whatever he would require!

I came home and spoke with Monique about the food plan. She told me that I had spent my career solving others' problems to make money and that I needed to use those analytical skills to solve my health problem that was tearing up our family. I looked her in the eyes, and I could just tell how much she was burdened by my injuries. It was taking a toll on her too. It was the first time I realized that she played the role of a "caregiver" in all of this, and like so many caregivers, she was fatigued. She was drained, so this time I didn't want to burden her even further. I lied and told her that I could figure this out when deep down, I had no idea where to start.

Chapter 5

When faced with adversity, you do what you're best at. For me,

*strategizing my path to healing was the **S.M.A.R.T** thing to do!*

I was restless the entire night but woke up the next morning with

enthusiasm. I was thankful for the life I had, and I knew that if I

could grow a successful business during the Great Recession,

then I could certainly figure "this" out! It's true that the situation

kept getting messier, but it was still in my hands to turn my fate

around. Thus, I bounced back, and using my analytical skills, ap-

proached the issue like any other business problem to solve:

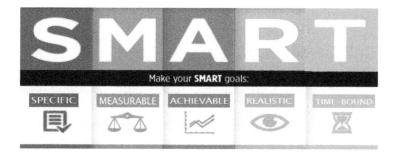

- *How did I define Victory* – achieving my end goal, which was to drop the weight and improve my A1C and other labs so I could have the surgery that would end my pain.

- What were the **S.M.A.R.T** goals to reach those objectives:
  - **Specific:** I would lose 40lbs, drop my A1C to below seven and achieve green indicators for the rest of my labs.
  - **Measurable**: I would take detailed measurements of my limbs, waist, chest, hips, and thighs, as well as record my weight every day. All other measurements would be taken weekly.
  - **Attainable**: I was in so much pain, so I could neither cook my own food nor do any of my usual activities to lose weight like Boxing, Biking, and Jogging. So, I planned to do the following:
    - Buy a proven meal plan where the food would be delivered and whose caloric intake would produce weight loss.

- Start using my YMCA gym membership. I would hire a swim coach to teach me how to swim without using my lower body and achieve a stroke that would eliminate the twisting associated with swimming.
- Lastly, I would change my schedule to accommodate my new "active schedule", so work no longer became an excuse for inactivity.

o **Relevant/Realistic**: This had to be a legitimate plan, so I would have Dr. "PCP's" approval on its ability to hit my goals. He stated that diet would be 90% of this problem, so I needed a plan that would train my body to eat five to six small meals a day and not exceed 1800 calories a day. Lastly, Dr. "PCP," told me to drink at least 64 ounces of water a day – perhaps closer to a gallon would be best.

o **Timely**: I would give myself four months to lose the weight; further, Dr. PCP would see me every six weeks to monitor my weight loss and laboratory indicators.

I did some research and found that Nutrisystem had a diet for people with a high A1C. This so-called Nutrisystem Plan for Men was not going to win any James Beard awards, but the frozen food was edible. There were five meals and dessert in the plan; damn, the chicken sandwich was smaller than my five-year-old's Happy Meal sandwich. The plan told me to add vegetables like tomatoes, lettuce, and pickle to every sandwich.

I then hired a swimming coach at the YMCA. Her name was Beth; she was about 5'10" and was the Aquatic Director at several YMCA facilities in Stone Mountain, GA. Swimming was tough because it engaged my lower body and caused severe pain. So, she put a floating board between my legs, which would keep them afloat, and taught me a modified breaststroke so my body would not twist during a swimming stroke.

Lastly, Beth taught me to always engage my core – it is like pulling in your lower waist to your lower spine when swimming. It took several weeks, but soon I was able to swim 100 meters without stopping. Also, I did not need the board anymore, so I was able to swim only using my arms and was able to keep my legs afloat by just engaging my core. It was a slow process, and I had 70-year-old women swimming around me while looking at me like I was a "Bitch." I did not care because I also noticed that my pain decreased when I was in the water. It was the only time of the day where my pain felt managed, where I could think and just be myself.

Monique suggested I also find a therapist that specializes in Pain Management. Monique told me that my pain was so visible that it reflected in my behavior, too, that it made me short-tempered and often depressed. That everyone at home and in the office had to walk on eggshells around me. Of course, I was aware of this and was constantly trying to monitor myself. But my wife was right; I did need someone to talk to regarding my pain that was here to stay. I needed someone who could give me good coping strategies on how to deal with it.

Chapter 6

Whatever you choose to do in life, do it with sheer determination. If you take up a task, take it with full responsibility and give your best to it. That's the only recipe for success; there are no shortcuts.

After working on my weight for the next two months, I visited Dr. Ortho for a check-up. After seeing my progress, she was quite impressed with my numbers. My B/P had come down to Dr. Ortho could not believe the progress I had made in just a matter of two months. This transformation had occurred from November through January – The Holiday Season.

For anyone who's tried to lose weight knows how difficult it is to reach your goal weight. Of course, it wasn't easy to hold me back. During this time, people usually tend to consume more as there are festivities going on, and everyone wants to have a good time with their families. I held myself back only for the sake of my health. Even Dr. Ortho was surprised and instantly asked how I accomplished this feat, and I walked her through my weight reduction process. I even showed her a picture of the Nutrisystem chicken sandwich. To be honest, it was a small portion of what I was used to eating. It wasn't enough for me, but I knew that's what I needed for a calorie deficit since I couldn't work out due to the pain.

"Is that all you eat?" Dr. Ortho was thoroughly shocked at the discovery.

"Well, I hook it up with lettuce, tomatoes, and pickles, but yes, this is a new reality," I said plainly.

Honestly, at this point, I was proud of myself too. When I saw my progress, it sort of motivated me to keep going on this way. She told me to keep up the good work and all I needed was a medical release for the surgery from my Dr. PCP.

I told my wife about the progress and the doctor's opinion on my current condition. She stated that it would probably take three months before they could take me in for the surgery as it would take some time for my A1C to be analyzed. I was heartbroken because I wanted the pain to stop, and the surgery was my ticket to a pain-free life. As for Dr. PCP, he liked my numbers too. He said it was a good start but gave me a look that "I was a long way" from getting a medical release. Thus, I went back into the pool and continued my diet with the Nutrisystem.

The pool hurt at first, but now it was the only time I did not feel any pain. I wish I could explain how peaceful it felt under the water. As for the sandwich, my body eventually learned to adapt to it as well. All I knew was that I enjoyed my swims and had to figure out how to work, swim, get my kids, and do Monique's "Honey Does." Miles had been a great help. His support meant a lot to me during that time. He never got mad that I missed soccer games or could not rough house with him the way we used to do in the past. He didn't even whine anymore when I asked him to pick up laundry or do groceries. He is a smart kid and knows how to take charge when needed, and I truly appreciate his efforts.

As for work, I did my best for as long as I could, but my anxiety continued to rise as things began to slip through the cracks. Monique was there to pick after me and to support me. She found an envelope with thousands of dollars from insurance payments that I forgot to deposit, and she was there to remind me about paydays when I forgot to sign the checks. She was practically there at every step and did not let my condition get in the way of work. Her constant reminders and her serious attitude towards our work were what kept me going.

I yelled, crying about this "Pill Brain" and feeling hopeless as I saw the years of legal and business craftmanship acquired during a lifetime of hard work, discipline, and a "never quit" attitude begins to erode by the pain medicine I took daily. Whenever I thought about the future, it would be blurry. I couldn't plan anything ahead as my brain was too focused on the constant pain. I would forget things, and it was getting to me because it was not normal at all. I was used to taking the proactive approach, but now I didn't even remember deadlines. My concerns were too apparent. Monique consoled me and stated the best thing for our business and family was for me to focus on my health.

Soon, I passed the 50lbs mark and stopped using Nutrisystem because I did not need it anymore -- It served its purpose by teaching me how to eat small portions, and it did wonders for me. Furthermore, Nutrisystem "broke" my "addiction" to food; and now, the meals stopped being about "joy" and became more about "fueling" the body. I learned that I should eat however much was needed for me to function.

Dr. PCP loved my progress. My A1C had also dropped to 6.7, and most of my numbers were green.

"Have you ever heard the term stretch goal?" he asked me.

"Yes, I've heard of the term," I replied confidently.

"Perfect," said Dr. PCP, *"then let's get this A1C below six and see if you can drop ten more pounds before I sign off on a surgery."*

"No problem," I stated with a smile. I couldn't believe that I was now closer to my surgery, and the whole time I wondered, *"How I could tweak my eating habits and swimming plan to hit these damn stretch goals."*

Chapter 7

We need to understand the importance of planning. Every important thing in life needs us to prepare beforehand. And the planning must be mindful. Going overboard with your plan does very little to get you where you want to be.

From the moment I took a dive into the swimming pool, it has given me nothing but peace. It was a change I never thought would work, but now it had become my new addiction as I hit 1000 meters and could swim double that length while still being far from tired. If anything, it energized me and revitalized my soul. It was the only time of the day when I felt that my pain was managed.

As I breathed and stroked through the water, the question of how to "tweak" my swimming plan was on top of my mind. What could I do to make it more efficient, something that would bring my A1C to 6?

I did my thinking, and my mind came up with what I do best – the **_S.M.A.R.T_** plan. This is what I had been doing all these years in business, I knew it worked, and it was the best way to turn things around in your favor.

- **Specific**: I knew exactly what my goal was. I needed to lose another 30lbs, drop my A1C to under 6.5, decrease my B/P to 120/80 and keep all other indicators green.

- It is truly a blessing to know what you want and where you're headed. Once your goal is clear, you can jump on to other stages.

- **Measurable**: I would record all my measurements and weight daily. My goals were measurable, so it was not a problem. I would check them often and make sure to record my numbers so I could always refer to them and see if I was making any progress at all.

- **Attainable**: My swimming plan needed to change. I needed a fiercer plan to get the numbers I had planned to achieve.

  - Swim 800 meters – 32 laps back and forth – in Wade Walker YMCA's 25-meter pool.

Wade Walker is a YMCA in Stone Mountain – It is a very diverse membership consisting of People of Color from across America,

Europe, Asia, and Africa. The Director's name is Lorna – an Asian American herself. In my opinion, they have the best pool and whirlpool in Dekalb County.

- Increase Swim Time – To 1000 meters at the same time it takes me to swim 800 meters, i.e., 30 minutes.

- 15 Minutes in Sauna – My medications make me retain water; thus, being in the Sauna helps me eliminate that water by sweating heavily.

- Increase Sweat Time – Add an additional 15 minutes in the Whirlpool for a combined 30 minutes of sweat time.

- Swim four days a week: Swimming was my only cardio, and I burned at least 300 calories per session. This was important as any form of physical exercise was out of the question for me.

- Increase swim time to five days a week – I would swim three days in a row, take a day off, then swim two days in a row. My caloric burn would increase with this goal as well, given the fact I would be swimming 200 meters more in my normal 30 minutes block of time.

As for my eating habits, my body was now accustomed to eating five small meals a day. From what I read, eating in small portions would help me burn fat and speed up my metabolism. The plan had to be easy, portable, and allow for the ability to swap out food while adhering to the same caloric count. After going through dozens of diabetic cookbooks, I developed a 1600 **Plug and Chuck** Meal Plan.

- **Relevant** – Dr. PCP had to approve my new Plug and Chuck Plan to see if it was relevant and would help me achieve my goal numbers.

We use the term "**Plug and Chuck**" in finance when we develop a model which easily allows for numbers to be swamped in and out and allows us to see the impact of those numbers. Here, I created an "Eating Model," which allowed me to swap out vegetables and proteins in a manner that kept me organized when counting calories. It was my hope that by enhancing both my swimming and eating plans, I could hit my weight loss target to obtain the surgery that would eventually stop my pain.

Dr. PCP gave me the "thumbs up" on my plan. He smiled at my determination and stated that he wished more of his patients were so "compliant" about their health. I think anyone walking around with the pain I had would do anything to get rid of it, and that's

what I was doing. My goal was to get the surgery done as soon as

I lost weight using my "KICK ASS" Eating Plan:

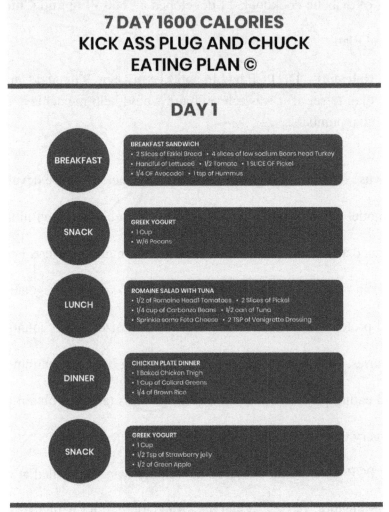

7 DAY 1600 CALORIES
KICK ASS PLUG AND CHUCK
EATING PLAN ©

DAY 1

BREAKFAST

BREAKFAST SANDWICH
- 2 Slices of Ezkiel Bread • 4 slices of low sodium Boars head Turkey
- Handful of Lettuce6 • 1/2 Tomato • 1 SLICE OF Pickel
- 1/4 OF Avocado1 • 1 tsp of Hummus

SNACK

GREEK YOGURT
- 1 Cup
- W/6 Pecans

LUNCH

ROMAINE SALAD WITH TUNA
- 1/2 of Romaine Head1 Tomatoes • 2 Slices of Pickel
- 1/4 cup of Carbonzo Beans • 1/2 can of Tuna
- Sprinkle some Feta Cheese • 2 TSP of Venigrette Dressing

DINNER

CHICKEN PLATE DINNER
- 1 Baked Chicken Thigh
- 1 Cup of Collard Greens
- 1/4 of Brown Rice

SNACK

GREEK YOGURT
- 1 Cup
- 1/2 Tsp of Strawberry jelly
- 1/2 of Green Apple

NO SALT EVERYTHING RUB (Vegetables)
• 1/2 TSP of Lemon Pepper • 1/2 TSP of Pepper • 1/4 TSP of Smoked Paprika
• 1/2TSP of Onion Powder • 1/2 TSP of Garlic Powder • 1 TSP of Mrs. Dash
• 1 TSP of Nutritional Yeast • 1/3 TSP of Mushroom Powder

7 DAY 1600 CALORIES
KICK ASS PLUG AND CHUCK
EATING PLAN ©

DAY 2

BREAKFAST

BREAKFAST SANDWICH
- 3 Egg Omelet • Mushrooms • Onions
- Diced Tomatoes • 2 Slices of Turkey Bacon
- 1 Slice of Ezikeil Bread

SNACK

GREEK YOGURT
- 1 Green Apple
- w/ 1 TSP Peanut Butter

LUNCH

ROMAINE SALAD WITH TUNA
- TUNA SALAD WRAP • 1/4 of Romaine Head • 1 tomato
- 2 slices of Pickel • 1/2 can of Tuna • Sprinkle some Feta Cheese
- 1 TSP of Mayo • 1 tsp of Hot Sauce • 1 Low Carb. Wrap

DINNER

CHICKEN PLATE DINNER
- Salmon Plate Dinner • 4 oz of Baked Salmon
- 1 cup of Broccoli • 1/2 Baked Potato

SNACK

GREEK YOGURT
- 1/2 SANDWICH • 1 Tsp of Peanut Butter

NO SALT EVERYTHING RUB (MEAT & Poultry)
- 1/2 TSP of Lemon Pepper • 1/2 TSP of Pepper • 1/2 TSP of Smoked Paprika
- 1/4 TSP of Onion Powder • 1/4 TSP of Garlic Powder • 1/4 TSP of Dry Mustard
- 1 TSP of Mrs. Dash • 1/3 TSP of Mushroom Powder • 1/4 Cup of Olive Oil
- 1/4 Cup of Balsamic Vinegar • 2 TSP of Texas Pete Hot Sauce

7 DAY 1600 CALORIES
KICK ASS PLUG AND CHUCK
EATING PLAN ©

DAY 3

BREAKFAST

BREAKFAST SANDWICH
- 1.5 Cups of Steel Cut Oatmeal • Dash of Cream
- 2 packs of splenda • 2 slices of Turkey Sausage

SNACK

GREEK YOGURT
- Avocado Toast • 1 Slice of Ezkeil Bread
- 1/4 Slice of Avocado • 1 TSP of Hummus

LUNCH

ROMAINE SALAD WITH TUNA
- CHICKEN PLATE DINNER • 1 BAKED CHICKEN THIGH
- 1 CUP OF BROCCOLI • 1/2 of Sweet Potato

DINNER

CHICKEN PLATE DINNER
- Spaghetti w/ Pasta • 4 ounces of low carb Noodles
- 1/4 of Spaghetti Sauce • 1 small salad

SNACK

GREEK YOGURT
- Apple w/ 1 tsp of Peanut Butter

NO SALT EVERYTHING RUB (FISH)
- 1/2 TSP of Lemon Pepper • 1/2 TSP of Pepper • 1/4 TSP of Mrs. Dash
- Juice of a lemon • 1/2 tsp of Mushroom Seasoning
- 1/4 cup of Olive Oil

7 DAY 1600 CALORIES
KICK ASS PLUG AND CHUCK
EATING PLAN ©

DAY 4

BREAKFAST

BREAKFAST SANDWICH
- 2 Slices of Ezkiel Bread • 4 slices of low sodium Boars head Turkey
- Handful of Lettuce8 • 1/2 Tomato • 1 SLICE OF Pickel
- 1/4 OF Avocado • 1 tsp of Hummus

SNACK

GREEK YOGURT
- 1 Cup • W/6 Pecans

LUNCH

ROMAINE SALAD WITH TUNA
- 1/2 of Romaine Head • 1 Tomatoes • 2 Slices of Pickel
- 1/4 cup of Carbonzo Beans • 1/2 can of Tuna
- Sprinkle some Feta Cheese • 2 TSP of Venigrette Dressing

DINNER

CHICKEN PLATE DINNER
- 1 Baked Chicken Thigh • 1 Cup of Collard Greens
- 1/4 of Brown Rice

SNACK

GREEK YOGURT
- 1 Cup • 1/2 Tsp of Strawberry jelly • 1/2 of Green Apple

7 DAY 1600 CALORIES
KICK ASS PLUG AND CHUCK
EATING PLAN ©

DAY 5

BREAKFAST

BREAKFAST SANDWICH
- 3 Egg Omelet • Mushrooms • Onions • Diced Tomatoes
- 2 Slices of Turkey Bacon • 1 Slice of Ezikeil Bread

SNACK

GREEK YOGURT
- 1 Green Apple • w/ 1 TSP Peanut Butter

LUNCH

ROMAINE SALAD WITH TUNA
- TUNA SALAD WRAP • 1/4 of Romaine Head • 1 tomato
- 2 slices of Pickel • 1/2 can of Tuna • Sprinkle some Feta Cheese
- 1 TSP of Mayo • 1 tsp of Hot Sauce • 1 Low Carb, Wrap

DINNER

CHICKEN PLATE DINNER
- Salmon Plate Dinner • 4 oz of Baked Salmon
- 1 cup of Broccoli • 1/2 Baked Potato

SNACK

GREEK YOGURT
- 1/2 SANDWICH • 1 Tsp of Peanut Butter

7 DAY 1600 CALORIES
KICK ASS PLUG AND CHUCK
EATING PLAN ©

DAY 6

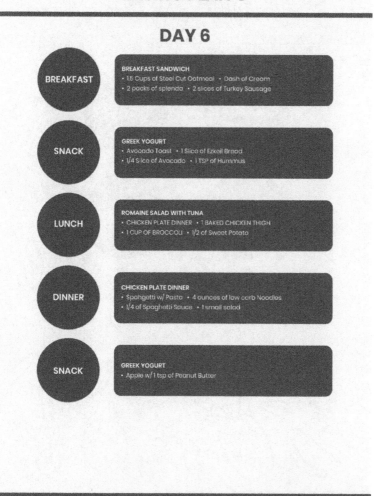

BREAKFAST

BREAKFAST SANDWICH
- 1.5 Cups of Steel Cut Oatmeal · Dash of Cream
- 2 packs of splenda · 2 slices of Turkey Sausage

SNACK

GREEK YOGURT
- Avocado Toast · 1 Slice of Ezkeil Bread
- 1/4 Slice of Avocado · 1 TSP of Hummus

LUNCH

ROMAINE SALAD WITH TUNA
- CHICKEN PLATE DINNER · 1 BAKED CHICKEN THIGH
- 1 CUP OF BROCCOLI · 1/2 of Sweet Potato

DINNER

CHICKEN PLATE DINNER
- Spahgetti w/ Pasta · 4 ounces of low carb Noodles
- 1/4 of Spaghetti Sauce · 1 small salad

SNACK

GREEK YOGURT
- Apple w/ 1 tsp of Peanut Butter

**7 DAY 1600 CALORIES
KICK ASS PLUG AND CHUCK
EATING PLAN ©**

DAY 7

CHEAT DAY

CHEAT DAY

CHEAT DAY

CHEAT DAY

Timely – I would give myself three months to drop the weight.

This is the most important part of any plan. I needed to give my-

self a deadline, so I wouldn't slack off any day. I needed to know that I only had three months to achieve my goals and reflect on my numbers. Once, I was done with S.M.A.R.T goals, it was now time to "Work My Plan!" The pain was enough to motivate me to work on it and get my life back on track.

Chapter 8

"**I LOVE IT**" when a plan comes together! – Colonel John "Hannibal" Smith – The A-Team 1983 to 1986"

"Jackson, I am getting my suitcase from Baggage Claim and will be out in a few minutes," my mother said on the phone while I waited at Hartsfield International Airport. Waiting, I thought about the events of the last month. "Your numbers are fantastic, Drs. PCP and Ortho stated:

- Weight: 350lbs -- 270lbs

- B/P: 190/130 -- 117/80

- A1C: 8.7 -- 5.8

- All Labs. Red – Green

Your transformation has been amazing, Mr. Dunbar, and it occurred in less than a year, Dr. Ortho," stated in a room with two other surgeons I had never seen before. I stated that it all came down to being **Anger-Focused!**

St. Patrick's Catholic School, 1979 – "Mommy, I did not cheat on the exam, and I don't know why Sister Mary Helen called you". I hated the principal's office; I've been "paddled" there at least twice this month for talking in class and my mom being called in from work meant my dad would be waiting for me with **Man Maker**" – his favorite belt. Nobody gave an ass "whopping" like my father. I saw "STARS" every time he used "**Man Maker**."

Hello Mrs. Dunbar, Jackson has been accused of cheating on his Math exam by his teacher.

"I did not cheat; I yelled; I worked hard studying for that easy exam when I could have been playing basketball with my friends". Sister Mary Helen looked at me with a scornful eye: "The penalty for cheating is expulsion!"

"My mother cut her off -- What proof do you have that Jackson cheated? Did anyone see him cheat?"

"No," stated Sister Mary Helen, "the teacher assumed he did because he got every question correct, and several of the concepts on the exam were barely touched on in class."

"So, you are saying my son got the top score in the class."

"Yes," stated Sister Mary Helen!

"So, if he retook the exam and got the same score, would you believe that he did not cheat?"

"This is a bunch of crap," I screamed, "why do I have to prove myself when I did nothing wrong?"

"Give us a few minutes; my mother asked Sister Mary Helen?"

When we were alone, my mother said:

"Listen, I believe you"! Your teacher is assuming you cheated because it is beyond her reason that a Black kid could outscore a room full of rich white kids. This is called **Institutional Racism** because this organization is acting unfairly toward you due to the color of your skin. It is time that you learn how to thrive when surrounded by people who have been taught that you are not as smart as they. It is not fair, and your father and I both deal with this every day, and it makes us angry as well."

"Here is what we do about it:

We get through the anger by being better at whatever we do. I am the best seamstress where I work, and your father is the supervisor's right-hand man, even though they won't promote him to that position. We use our Anger as a source of strength when confronted with racism, and now, you must do the same".

Jackson, ***Anger unchecked will lead you to a path ending in jail or worse.*** But, ***<u>Anger-Focused on your goals</u>*** will give you the strength to break down any door – called Institutional Racism -- that stands in your way. When you retake the exam:

- Think about the embarrassment you felt being called a cheater in class.

- Think about the fear you had about how I would react.

- Take all that Anger and focus it on the exam.

See yourself getting every question correct and walking into that class with your head held high. Always remember, you will have to deal with these "Doors" called Institutional Racism your entire life; use ***Anger-Focused*** to go through them, around them, above them, and under them to reach your goals!

One hour later, Mrs. Dunbar, your son received another perfect score; he can go back to class now. My mom yelled, "I demand the teacher apologies to him in front of all the other students immediately"! I walked back to class thinking about "**Anger Focused**," not knowing that it would be my Superpower to knock down walls all the way to the current day. **Anger-Focused was how I completed my body transformation in less than six months! Anger-Focused** on:

- The driver who carelessly hit me changed my life forever.
- All the pain I endured kept me from playing with my kids and being intimate with my wife.

- The embarrassment of having Dr. Ortho say on a speakerphone that my family could hear, "It was my fault I was in pain"!

I took all that ***Anger and Focused*** it on my resolve to lose the weight by clean eating and exercising even though I was in pain. I could see my body being leaner, see myself dancing with my wife, and **Anger-Focused** made it happen.

Me @ 270 right before surgery

"Mr. Dunbar, you have a herniated disk that is impacting on a nerve, and this is causing you pain. We will perform a Laminectomy – A procedure that removes the portion of the vertebra near the nerve; and, in doing so, stops your pain. The procedure will take about four hours and the recovery about six weeks. Your surgery is scheduled for April 26, 2016, as I just received the approval letter from Dr. PCP."

I love it when a plan comes together! My family went out to dinner and celebrated the coming of the surgery and my new body. While chewing my entrée salad with lite vinaigrette on the side, the news of my surgery date all seemed so anti-climactic. I had months to plan, so things were good at the office, and mom was coming to help at home. All I good do is just pray and hope the doctors could deliver a "pain ending" surgery as I had delivered a body "more than fit" for surgery – only time would tell?

Chapter 9

"Everybody has a plan until they get punched in the mouth. At this point, you can "roll" with the punches or opt to never get off the mat" – Mike Tyson.

My mother flew up to Atlanta to help us with the kids and was shocked at how much weight I had lost. Father Greg, my Pastor from Holy Trinity Parish, came to the hospital and gave me a kind blessing. My wife and I then went to a hospital room, and I changed into a gown. The Anesthesiologist came and said my pressure was a little high. I started breathing exercises and begged him to still do the procedure. I looked at Monique, and then suddenly, Dr. "Ortho" was standing over me, saying the surgery went well. I could not believe it was over just like that!

I laid in bed, and I was in a lot of pain. Pain in my back, leg/foot, and groin. They kept pushing fluids as well. I was very dizzy and could not move. Rehab took one looked at me and stated they could not work with me. My wife was laughing. She stated, "stupid stuff was coming out my mouth without me real-izing." Monique decided to stay with me every night I was in the hospital. I could hear her reviewing my charts with my clinical team.

Suddenly, my friend Howard came into my room and stayed with me most of the day. My mom always told me that you discover who your friends are when you are at your lowest point. He had been waiting with Monique and told me the surgery lasted almost four hours. The surgeon came in and said everything went well and that I should recover in about six weeks. There was all this pressure in my groin, and it really hurt: Like I had to urinate, but I could not do so. The nurse came in and stated they would have to put a catheter in me to relieve the pressure. She asked Monique to hold me down as she inserted the device so I could urinate. I began to laugh and thanked them for the early present as my Birthday was in a few days. My wife asked why did I thank her? I stated that I always wanted two on one action, and now I was getting it, though this was not what I imagined.

My home was not built for people with mobility issues. It is a Craftsman-inspired home, which means it is on a narrow lot and built high like a townhome. Stated another way, we had a lot of high steps – 14 of them -- and no bedroom or full bathroom on the main level. For this reason, we ordered a hospital bed, urinal, and porta potty for the downstairs. I was told the rest and practice walking to and from my door for the first week. The pain in my lower back had decreased as did the nerve pain; but I still felt pain. I would call Dr. Ortho's nurse a few times and she told me not to overdo it, stay in bed, take a break and that they would see me in five to six weeks.

I soon received a letter from BCBS denying the hospital claim. Emory told me not to worry about it until I got a bill from them. I hate insurance companies. You pay your premiums every month with the understanding that if you get sick, they will hold up their end, and pay for the health procedures. The issue is too many of these companies deny claims so they can pocket billions of dollars in premiums in the form of profits. They just piss on the little man, and it was not right!

I felt better when I went back to Dr. Ortho and was cleared to begin swimming and rehab. I was able to begin working with "PT" again, she was surprised at the new me as I had lost 75lbs by that time. I also began swimming, but my foot went number when I began to engage my lower body.

I would also see Dr. PCP. He was not happy that I missed my last appointment and did not like one of my medications: Valium and Oxycodone are "Schedule II" narcotics and were addictive Opioids. I told him about the pain, and he stated I should see Emory's Pain Management group as they were great at their job. I told him that I was still having erection issues, and he prescribed Cialis.

I selected Dr. Pain-Free as my pain management person because she went to an excellent Medical School with more than 20 years of experience. She was also an African American medical provider. Dr. Pain-Free did some rotation movements with my leg, and we talked about weening me off Oxycodone and Valium by:

- Increase my dosage of Gabapentin.
- Place me on Tramadol.
- Start on Cymbalta for nerve pain.

This was a stressful time, and for whatever reason, my nerve and low back pain came back with a vengeance. Further, my insurance company denied the Cymbalta medication and refused to pay my hospital expenses, which met I had to fight while being undermedicated. Worse, no one on my pain management team would increase my meds because they did not believe I was in pain. They stated the surgery should have worked and that MRI scans did not show anything wrong.

As I worked in the medical field, I became ANGRY, knowing

the "float game" BCBS was playing. ALWAYS read the **Expla-**

nation of Benefits "E.O.B" letter – as it tells your medical costs

for a procedure, then:

- Open the letter.

- Find "provider and patient responsibility" in the middle of

  the page.

- Check the MATH! Make sure the insurance company

  calculates what you owe correctly; for example – Procedure

  costs = $20,000:

  - Insurance Pays 80% after a $4000 deductible; then

    patient responsibility = $4000 + (20% *20,000) or

    8000

- o Insurance Pays 80% for an in-network provider, but 60% for an out of network provider and your doctor is out of network; after a $4000 deductible; then patient responsibility = ($4000 + (40% * 20,000) or $12,000.

Most people don't catch mistakes on their EOBs for months. This allows health insurance companies to hold on to **Billions** of dollars in cash for a longer period – making **interests or investments** from money that should be used to pay your bills. In the end, these issues could take up to a year to resolve, and here I was trying to solve them in real-time. Insurance companies are nothing but pyramid schemes.

I read my "E.O.B form and called my insurer to pay these claims correctly with the utmost of speed. My insurer then miscalculated my deductible. Each time I caught one of their mistakes, they said it would take 30 to 45 days to fix, which met I was on the hook for all the medical bills.

I spent months fighting with BCBS to pay my medical bills:

- First, they denied the claim.

- Then BCBS paid the Hospital as an out-of-network provider, which meant I would pay at least twice as much.

- Finally, they paid the claim correctly after six months of fighting.

Work became harder as well as the pain was all-consuming, it became harder to focus during negotiations, and I started making mistakes that cost "real" money. It was harder to manage staff as I would often repeat myself or get lost in conversation. At this time, WellMed/Atlanta had grown every year, with 2016 being our best year; but I worried for the future as I could not venture out and prospect for corporate sales accounts anymore.

I could not sleep and fell, screaming in front of my kids. I lied to them and said I was fine, but they knew I was lying – it was the lowest point in my life. I turned to drink vodka – Stolis – and drank it until the pain went away. I lived this way for three months, and no Pain Doctor I spoke with would increase my pain medication.

Monique was a blessing during this time as she helped me deal with these stressors. She was finally convinced we needed to scale back our corporate medical placement program and non-medical operations and end all sales/marketing until I was fit enough to manage the tasks. **In essence, I left the company that I started to focus exclusively on my health.** Yes, that would be a serious hit to our bottom line; but that was far safer than creating a bigger enterprise that was not well managed due to my existing pain.

Chapter 10

Sometimes you do everything right in life and still don't get

where you want to. Don't lose hope. If you've come this far,

you'll find the strength to move further ahead.

Having done everything I was supposed to, I still found myself in

immense pain. I told Dr. Pain-Free that I could not understand

why the pain had not gone away since hitting all of Emory's goals:

- Lose 40lbs – I lost almost 20% of my body weight, or over

  80lbs.

- Get my A1C under 7.0 – It was a 5.7 on my last visit.

- Have most of my numbers under control.

- Changed eating habits.

As someone who couldn't wait to get rid of the pain, I had done

everything according to the plan. I not only managed to surpass

but also "CRUSHED" every metric they gave me. That's how I

was able to get my surgery done, yet I was still in pain. I felt like I was going crazy most of the time!

Dr. Pain-Free was able to get my insurance company to authorize the Cymbalta, which did little to help manage my nerve pain. The drug also made me sick and increased my "Pill Brain." This went on for about two weeks, but the increase in Pill Brain continues to this day.

She also wanted to do an MRI with contrast dye would be injected into my body, which would improve the imaging of the scans.

I also tried going to other Pain Management Doctors, and they would either not take me on as a patient or, if they did, they wouldn't change my pain medications. I even went to a Dentist one day with a broken tooth; the pain was terrible! When they discovered I was a pain patient, the nurse would only prescribe Advil "Ibuprofen" for pain management for the two weeks until my next appointment. So, the next time I made sure I didn't mention that I was a pain patient, and that did not work. I was going insane and wanted to hurt something, yet none of the so-called medical professionals seemed to give a damn!

Monique started hiding my pain history would not work at all because of the **Prescription Drug Monitoring Program of Georgia** (PDMP) – an electronic database used to monitor the prescribing and dispensing of controlled substances. It provides prescribers and pharmacists with critical information regarding a patient's-controlled substance prescription history.

This was "Big Brother" for medications! All the medications prescribed to me up until that point were in this database. Once my pain management history was discovered, no Pain Medicine Doctor would touch me or change my current medication dosages. In the end, it seemed like every other MD looked at me with a deliberate suspicious eye.

Going to the Pharmacy was far worse. The Pharmacists looked at me as if I was trying to steal something. They always wanted to know why I was taking the medication, why my doctor's office was 20 miles away, then demanded that I call the office to verify I was a patient. I felt racially profiled and told her to call the provider her DAMN self! It was infuriating the way these medical "professionals" treated me.

The pharmacist was adamant about calling the doctor, and sometime later, she handed me the phone. My doctor on the other side of the line stated, "Mr. Dunbar, you were a **BMWSII!**"

This meant I was a **Black Man with a Schedule II** opioid drug, and the Pharmacist was hassling me because she did not believe my medication was valid. My doctor was also mad because the Pharmacist demanded proof that my provider was legitimate. I had faced these inconveniences numerous times while I was on pain medication.

Anyway, soon I got the MRI results in which Dr. Pain-Free had found that I had scar tissue around the incision of my surgery. She then diagnosed me with *Post Laminectomy Syndrome* or *Failed Back Surgery Syndrome.* It was a scary situation for me; I didn't know what stood for me next. The good news was that my pain medication would be increased, but the bad news was that there was no cure for scar tissue: I would be in Chronic Pain for the rest of my life!

The doctor gave me three surgical treatment options:

A steroid injection:

- This would only give short term relief and cost roughly around $2,100.

Promised:

- Immediate relief, which meant it was cost-effective.

My Results:

- Relief was temporary and lasted for about five weeks, shorter every time a shot was given.

Radiofrequency:

- They would burn the area around the nerves granting pain relief, and cost roughly around $4500.

- **Promised**: Pain relief for up to 12 months.

- **My results**: Pain score dropped from 9 to 4 for six weeks, and then full acute pain returned.

Spinal Cord Stimulator Implant:

- "A Pacemaker" for the spine would be "hardwired to my spine, possessing wires protruding from my body and attaching to a device on my hip. This device would trick my brain into thinking it was not in pain and cost $30,000 to 50,000.

- *Promised*: Pain Relief for years.

- ***Research Found***: Up to three months recovery time and has a failure rate of 25% to 30%

I thanked her for the information and was relieved that there were ways to get out of this situation. It was good to know that finally, someone believed me, but then I asked, "why not just increase my medications?" I did not receive an answer to my question, as she doubled down on the surgical treatment options as this seemed to be her preferred method for addressing pain. It then hit me that I should have asked Dr. Pain-Free about her treatment philosophy, as surgical treatments cost money and often cause painful recovery. Whether or not a provider believes in surgical methods, aggressive medications, or alternative remedies for addressing Chronic Pain is a question every Chronic Pain patient should ask before bringing a provider on their Wellness team?

I gave Dr. Pain-Free a hug, as the Steroid Injection – one of many – had me almost pain-free during the Christmas Holidays. I took that time to proffer the query:

Why did no one believe I needed better Pain Management despite years of evidence like proof of nerve damage in my medical files?

It just didn't make any sense. It was clear that I had been in pain for a long time, yet no doctor seemed to be talking about increasing my dosage. It felt like I was just cut off from substantive Pain Management after my surgery, and I needed to know the cause. I needed to attack this problem like any other business or legal question:

- **Why had it happened to me?**
- **Is it happening to other people as well?**
- **What measures could I take to improve my quality of care?**

Chapter 11

My Hypothesis:

Race Matters in Pain Medicine! As a result, we are left with the critical under-medication of African Americans, who suffer with unbearable Chronic Pain and the severe over-medication of White Americans, which helped cause the Opioid Crisis.

Opioids are a class of drugs naturally found in the opium poppy plant that works in the brain to produce a variety of effects, including the relief of pain with many of these drugs.

Opioids can be prescription medications often referred to as painkillers, or they can be so-called street drugs, such as heroin. Many prescription opioids are used to block pain signals between the brain and the body and are typically prescribed to treat moderate to severe pain. In addition to controlling pain, opioids can make some people feel relaxed, happy, or "high" and can be addictive. Additional side effects can include slowed breathing, constipation, nausea, confusion, and drowsiness.

Nearly 200 Americans die each day from a drug overdose. In August 2018, the NIDA reported that there were more than 70,000 drug overdose deaths in the United States in 2017. This is more than four times the rate of overdose deaths in 1999. Drug overdoses are now the leading cause of death for Americans under the age of 50 years:

DEATH-DATA	2010 - 2015	2016	2017	2018	2019	2010-2019 #
Opioids Death	153,820	42,249	47,600	46,802	49,860	340,331
All Drug Overdose Deaths	264,612	63,632	70,237	67,367	70,630	536,478
						-
Opioids as % of all Drug Deaths	58%	66%	68%	69%	71%	63%

Abuse of opioids resulted in a 493% increase in the rate of opioid use disorder between 2010 and 2016: with prescription medications making up 66% of overdose cases. Further, during the last two decades, the suburbs have become ground zero for heroin use, involving primarily White women and men in their late 20s. Interestingly, is that 75% of heroin users in treatment started their opioid misuse with prescription analgesics.

Chronic Pain affects **50 million** U.S. adults and "High Impact" Chronic Pain -- which interferes with life or work activities -- impact **20 million** people. Roughly one month before my surgery in 2016, President Barack Obama's CDC issued guidelines advising primary care doctors to prescribe opioids as a last resort for pain and then in the lowest effective doses. The guidance also "suggested" a three-day limit for initial prescriptions for acute pain and recommended avoiding prescribing increasing large doses for those complaining of Chronic Pain – defined as pain not associated with cancer or cancer-associated therapies that persist *beyond three to six months*.

This was alarming news! As a Chronic Pain patient, one finds that the effectiveness of pain medications abates when your body becomes accustomed to the dosage. My surgery was in April of 2016; before that time, my medications would be increased to fit my pain level. Now, the current federal guidelines were telling doctors to stop that practice, which would lead to the under medication of pain patients.

Donald Trump's campaign to "cut" the Opioid Crisis by cutting prescriptions by one-third over a three-year period. He also sought stepped-up prosecutions of doctors who prescribe inappropriately and tougher sentences for those who sell drugs illegally. His administration also invested billions in prevention, treatment, and research and authorized respected science groups to develop better guidelines for doctors safely treat patients with severe pain. Who were these people suffering from opioid addiction and/or overdose?

DEATH-DATA	2010	2016	2017	2018	2019	2010-2019 #	%
White	127,527	33,450	37,113	35,363	35,977	269,430	80%
Black Non Hispanic	11,402	4,374	5,513	6,088	7,464	34,841	10%
Other	14,891	4,425	4,974	5,351	6,419	36,060	10%
Total Opioids Deaths	153,820	42,249	47,600	46,802	49,860	340,331	100%

The above charts show that 80% of those who have died from Opioids Deaths from 2010 to 2019 were White Men and Women. Stated another way, most of the billions being invested for treatment, prevention, and new groundbreaking research were going to White Women and Men in their late 20s, representing the majority of Heroin and Opioid users. Although I am a middle-aged Black Man who does not fit the profile of a heroin or opioid abuser, that did/does not stop me from being profiled by medical providers and pharmacists alike.

I thought about the *"War on Drugs"* during the late 80's and '90s: A time when "CRACK" cocaine was running wild, destroying lives and communities as millions became addicted to the drug. I also remembered as a child watching Nancy Reagan on "Different Strokes" tell me to "Just Say No Campaign" to get tough on drugs – it was inspiring. Surely those addicted to "CRACK" received the same treatment as those addicted to Opioids -- The answer was NO!

In the 1980s, President Ronald Reagan's "War on Drugs" made a link between minorities, drugs, and crime in the American rhetoric. Media hysteria about an unsubstantiated crack epidemic amongst minorities prompted Congress to pass draconian mandatory minimum sentences:

- Possession of 500 grams of powder cocaine = five years in prison.

- Possession of 5 grams of Crack = 5 years in prison.

- The judge's discretion in sentencing was removed = Automatic Prison.

- One strike law evicts residents from Public Housing if any drugs are found.

- Lifetime ban on welfare benefits for anyone with a drug conviction.

Even though Whites outnumber Blacks five to one, represent most of the Crack users and Dealers, and both groups use and sell drugs at similar rates; African Americans compromised:

- 35% of those arrested for drug possession.

- 55% of those convicted for drug possession.

- 74% of those convicted for drug possession.

The statistics for the Latino population were equally disturbing. Latinos comprise 12.5% of the population and use and sell drugs less than whites, yet they accounted for 46% of those charged with a federal drug offense in 1999.

Law enforcement practices fuel racial inequalities in the criminal justice system. Over the years, the Drug Enforcement Administration (DEA) has helped train police to profile highway travelers for potential drug couriers. This profile is based on associating People of Color with crime, creating a phenomenon known as "Driving While Black or Brown."

In Maryland, for instance, although only 21% of drivers along a stretch of Interstate 95 are Minorities, including Blacks, Latinos, Asians, and others, 80% of those who are pulled over and searched are People of Color. In California, between 80% and 90% of all motorists arrested by law enforcement officials since 1991 have been members of minority groups. These statistics are not the product of chance but of purpose and can be found throughout the country.

Enforcement and Punishment were the treatment plans for Minorities addicted to Crack, filling prisons -- with **Modern-Day**

Slavery being the result! A vicious cycle of incarceration, addiction, and helplessness with little compassion or assistance from the government: <u>**The opposite of what White people addicted to Opioids get today**</u>!

I became even angrier "crunching" the data on Opioid Deaths thinking of all the providers and pharmacists who saw my "Black' face in their minds' eye when thinking of drug abusers, instead of the under 30-year-old White female and male demographic making up to 80% of Opioid deaths. Then I noticed an interesting trend:

DEATH-DATA	2016		2017		2018		2019	
White	33,450	79%	37,113	78%	35,363	76%	35,977	72%
Black Non Hispanic	4,374	10%	5,513	12%	6,088	13%	7,464	15%
Other	4,425	10%	4,974	10%	5,351	11%	6,419	13%
Total Opioids Deaths	42,249		47,600		46,802		49,860	

Opioid deaths of White women and men seemed to peak at around 80%, dropping to 72% in 2019, while African American death by Opioid drugs seemed to increase from 10% to 15% during the same period. As an African American Chronic Pain patient, I needed to understand why this increase occurred?

I thought about being taken off Oxycodone and Valium after my surgery and going thru withdrawal because no one would increase my pain medication, as they did not believe I was still in pain. I was undermedicated, in terrible pain, and desperate for anything that would relieve my suffering. Were there other African Americans subjected to the same brand of inequitable Pain Medicine, and if so, did that contribute to the above-listed opioid deaths?

I went off my medications to have a clear head during my research– which meant I would be in great pain -- and found that African Americans are systematically under-treated for pain because of "outdated" stereotypes going back to Slavery. That the skin of African Americans is thicker than white people's skin, thereby making African Americans more impervious to pain and White people less.

A 2016 study of White medical students found that 50% of the participants endorsed these beliefs. These participants also rated Black (vs. White) patients' pain as lower and made less accurate treatment recommendations. The findings of this study suggest that individuals with some medical training hold and may use false beliefs about biological differences between Black and Whites to inform medical judgments, which contribute to racial inequity in pain management.

This idea of Black people experiencing less pain than White people were also an idea started from 19th-century experiments conducted on slaves by a physician named Thomas Hamilton. A wealthy plantation owner tortured an enslaved Black man named John Brown, creating blisters all over his body to prove Black skin went deeper than White skin.

How does this stereotype impact medical treatment? A 2019 study published in the American Journal of Emergency Medicine found Black patients were 40 less likely to receive medication for acute pain compared to White patients and 32% less likely to be prescribed opioids. The gap was largest when the cause of the pain, such as back pain, was not immediately apparent. Another survey suggests that doctors – nationwide, about 72% are White – often underestimate the pain level of minority patients.

I was shocked reading these statements and then began to fear for my Black wife and Black children. How did this inequity in Pain Medicine impact my Black wife when seeking pain relief and my Black children when they got sick or had to visit an Emergency Room for a pain-related injury?

I discovered that Dr. James Marion Sims, known as the father of gynecology, conducted experimental surgeries on enslaved Black women without anesthesia, developing a body of work that misrepresents how Black women experience pain.

The thought is that Black women are not educated about their own bodies, stated Dr. Colene Arnold – A gynecologist specializing in pelvic pain disorder. Dr. Arnold pointed to a study finding Black women are less likely to be diagnosed with endometriosis than White women when experiencing pelvic pain. Instead, Black women are misdiagnosed as having a sexually transmitted pelvic inflammatory disease.

A more current study completed by Dr. Green of the Departments of Population Health Sciences and Obstetrics & Gynecology at the University of Wisconsin-Madison was presented at the 2020 Society for Maternal-Fetal Medicine Conference. Dr. Green and her team found that "Black patients reported higher average levels of pain compared to White patients, but still received similar amounts of pain medication."

Controlling for reported pain scores, explained to Dr. Green, Black patients received less pain medication than their White counterparts. This was also true of Asian patients. The team also analyzed pain medication prescriptions from 310 health systems

that provide primary care to Black and White patients. They

found that, overall, Black and White's patients were equally

likely to be given prescriptions for pain relief. The difference

was in the dosages prescribed. As 90% of the healthcare

systems monitored in the study found White patients received

higher doses on an annual basis than Black patients. In most of

these systems, the difference in prescription dosage strength was

15% or greater.

As for my beautiful Black children who frequent the Emergency

Room due to sports-related soccer and dance injuries: Black

children are significantly less likely to receive pain medications

when compared to their white counterparts.

Tiffani Johnson, MD, and her team analyzed 2006-2009 from the

National Ambulatory Medical Care Survey conducted by the

Centers for the Disease Control and National Center for Health

Statistics. Their findings were disturbing: Black and Hispanic

children were more likely to stay in an Emergency Room six

hours longer than White kids and receive significantly less pain treatment than White kids even when rating their pain at a seven or higher on a 10-point scale.

Remembering the times my daughter cried in pain while receiving treatment in the Emergency Room, I read that Black children with acute appendicitis – a pain emergency – are less likely than white children to receive painkillers. Black children with moderate pain were less likely to receive any analgesia, and Black children with severe pain were less likely to be treated with opioids.

These findings came from a national survey of 900,000 children with acute appendicitis. They found only 57% of Black kids received anything for their pain in the emergency room, only 41% got any opioid drugs, and just 12% of Black children got any opioid drugs for pain, despite opioids being strongly recommended for appendicitis. There is another term for this "bias" in Pain Medicine treatment: **Institutional Racism**! And I wondered if the

Opioid crackdown made things worse for Chronic Pain Black patients?

American physicians wrote over 255 million prescriptions for opioid pain relievers in 2012. As part of the "War on Opioids," the CDC and other federal and state lawmakers focused on significantly decreasing prescribing and usage. By 2020, there was only 142 million opioids prescription; and the methods used to accomplish this feat came from some of the 2016 CDC guidelines for Prescribing Opioids for Chronic Pain:

- Nonpharmacologic therapy and nonopioid therapy are preferred for Chronic Pain patients.
- Establish treatment goals, next steps, and completion with a patient before starting opioid therapy.
- When opioids are started, clinicians should prescribe the lowest effective dosage.

In following these recommendations, some doctors prescribed ineffective over-the-counter medicines and talk therapies instead of opioids for patients with serious injuries, despite there being

no scientific basis for concluding that nondrug treatments are an

adequate substitute for opioids when controlling severe pain.

While others just discontinued prescribing Opioids or "aggres-

sively "tapered" their patients from the use of Opioid drugs.

Caused by one recent study of 100,000 pain patients who were

tapered from Opioids: An 68% increase in overdoses and a

100% increase in mental health concerns.

Furthermore, one study found up to 30% of all "accidental"

overdoses are "suicides by opioids" due to chronic pain patients

being aggressively tapered from their opioids. Now, if we apply

that "factor' to the below Opioid Death Chart:

	2016	2017	2018	2019	2010-2019	
Assumed 30% - "Suicide by Opioids"						
White	10,035	11,134	10,609	10,793	80,829	80%
Black Non Hispanic	1,312	1,654	2,239	2,239	10,452	10%
Other	1,328	1,492	1,926	1,926	10,818	10%
Total Opioids Deaths	12,675	14,280	14,774	14,958	102,099	100%

We have – as of 2019, over 102,000 suicides that could have been labeled "accidental overdoses: with an "upward trend" of suicides occurring with Black Chronic Pain patients.

Think about the medical studies:

- With 50% of medical students believing that Black skin is thicker than white skin, this mindset led to no pain medication being given to Black patients or fewer opioids in the best case.

  - Black patients are 40% less likely to receive pain medication for acute pain and 32% less likely to get opioids for chronic pain.

  - With 90% of White patients receiving higher dosages (15% and greater) for pain management than Black patients?

If you then tell me that opioid prescriptions written by American Physicians dropped from 255 million to 142 million due to following strict tapering guidelines and fears of liability; then I ask you:

- Were the opioid medications of African Americans unfairly and disproportionally stopped?

- Were African American Acute and Chronic Pain patients unfairly and disproportionally denied opioid medicine that would have improved their lives?

- If so, did this **Institutional Racism** produce a miserable quality of life for African American pain patients, causing a **disproportional number** of opioid overdoses and/or **"suicides by opioids"** in the Black community?

- Lastly, did this **Institutional Racism** produce a miserable quality of life for White Americans, as their prescriptions for higher doses of opioids led to addiction, destruction of communities, and became a cause of the Opioid Crisis?

In 2019 the CDC stated **"OOOOPS,"** its guidelines were being abused by governmental and medical institutions, causing the above listed "unintended consequences," but failed to take any action. The CDC is expected to release a revised guideline on opioid prescribing in 2022; in the meantime, "we Chronic Pain" patients are on our own.

Race Matters in Pain Medicine: I said, screaming to my mother over the phone! My mother worked two jobs most of my childhood to keep food on the table and a roof over our heads. I was so proud to be her son, and she remains the hardest working and kindest person I've ever known.

My mom listened to every word, then said, "Do you remember when you were a kid back in Catholic School?" Yes, I said. "And that teacher accused you of cheating, and the principal believed her." Yes, I said.

"Do you remember what I taught you?"

"Of course, I do, mom: **AngerFocused** on a goal that I can fully see in my mind's eye was the way to fight Institutional Racism. I've used **AngerFocused** to go under, to go above and to go around, to go through that "Door" called Institutional Racism my whole life."

"Then, my son, take a deep breath and use **Anger Focused** to improve your quality of life. Jackson, you always knew that "Life was unfair,"; and that never stopped you from being successful. Yes, life is unfair, so why would that be any different for Pain Medicine?! So, my question, Jackson: **What are you going to do about it?"**

Chapter 12

Real Men, Especially Real Black Men
Do Not Get Therapy?

My body was functioning on just a few hours of restless sleep at night which was not enough to understand my mother's statements. There was a lot of anxiousness in me that had to be comprehended before I could make use of the "Anger Focus" process to bring some betterment in my life and behavior. But it all had to take time, and I knew that, but maybe that time of betterment was not today as I completely lost my temper and yelled at the Teller today in the bank for absolutely no reason.

I felt like my body was under someone else's control and that someone was not me but my anger which was making its way out of my body without any solid reason. My brain was under so much stress, and my feelings were all over the place, but it was not Teller's fault. So why did I yell at her? Why did I make her feel worst about the situation? I could feel she feared me now, but the damage was done.

I wanted to calm myself, too, so I called Monique out of embarrassment. I told her everything that had happened and how ashamed I was of myself.

"Call Dr. Pain-Free; nobody can get you through this but her. I'm sure she has something for you, perhaps an increase in Cymbalta dosage, which wouldn't be of any harm."

I could feel Monique's word penetrating through my ears and hurting me, but I knew she was right, and she was doing it for me, to bring peace to my life and curb my depression through my medications for my own sake. I had been on Cymbalta for some time now as they helped me with my mental health and depression. So, I decided to talk to Dr. Pain-Free about Monique's suggestion. To my surprise, Dr. Pain-Free wasn't too happy with the idea.

"Jackson, there could be stark complications!" I stared blankly at Dr. "Pain-Free" as she talked.

"Increased dosage of Cymbalta might cause a seizure in your brain if it is mixed with other painkillers."

She was trying to knock some sense in a grownup, desperate man who needed nothing but the cure.

"I'm sorry, but I cannot increase your dosage," She finally said.

"Then why did I yell at her? Why do I keep hurting people with my behavior?" I found myself questioning her in a firm but broken voice?

"Dr. Pain-Free, I'm a big Black man; I cannot be the one yelling at people, as it would bring bad consequences. I just want to be my old self, who was calm in every situation and even kept others calm too. The person who was calm at the time of his own accident two years ago." This time, there was pleading in my voice.

I had confused Dr. Pain-Free, but she listened to me carefully and removed me from Tramadol, which was my strongest pain relief medicine, only to increase my Cymbalta to help with my mood swings.

Thus, I had two options:

- Decrease my pain meds, and increase my mental health meds, which would cure my mood swings, but I would be in more pain.

- Make no change to my medications, and the erratic behavior would continue

Either way, I was screwed. But I had to make a choice. Perhaps the most difficult one. So, with a heavy heart, I decided on the first option. But still, I needed a gateway from my miserable behavior. Monique had strongly suggested an experienced therapist. Being a Psychiatrist herself, she helped me push back the idea of "Only weak men need therapy," which **every** Black man was taught growing up.

Monique wanted a genuine therapist for me who had experience in his field.

"You have a lot of thin-skinned therapists with less than five years of experience, passing themselves off as experts. They would not be a good fit!" She spoke. I knew she wasn't wrong.

"Jack trust me! I have come across all types during my 20-year career. I have treated people who were sexual offenders, and racists during that time." I knew there was no lie in what she was saying.

"I just want you to know that an experienced therapist is important for you at this point because you have symptoms of depression, mood swings, forgetfulness, and irritability, which means you need an expert who has experience in dealing with patients with traumas, someone who knows Pain Management and the impact of medications. Maybe a Psychologist or Psychiatrist, perhaps both?" Monique looked at me with hope.

She then gave me a list of five "seasoned" therapists that our WellMed/Atlanta team put together: The name at the top was Dr. Feelings, PhD.

A few days later, an old childhood friend Tommy was in town, and I took him to have drinks and cigars at the Stone Mountain Public House, one of my favorite places. I loved this charming cigar bar. It reminds me of many of the pubs I visited in Germany and France during my extended time in Europe. Besides that, the live Jazz Music always puts me at ease, and the smell of Cigar Smoke and good food make the ***Stone Mountain Public House "Cigar & Piano" Bistro*** my favorite local pub.

"This is a great place, Jack thanks for showing me Atlanta today." I could tell Tommy was delighted to see the finest pub and me in Atlanta.

"No worries, Tommy. I haven't seen you in years, so I am glad you missed your layover as it gave us time to catch up," I said.

Tommy and I met when I moved to Pleasantville, New Jersey, after my parents' divorce. Tommy and his brother Mike were one of the few White kids that went to Pleasantville High, and they were always getting bullied. Maybe that is why I connected with Tommy. Coming from a middle school and being the only African

American kid, I knew what it was like to get hassled on the playground. There was one difference between our experiences: Tommy never had to prove himself to teachers; I always did!

"So, you've been talking to me all day about the data you found on Institutional Racism in Pain Medicine? Why did you start the research?" Tommy's voice brought me out of nostalgia which I was having at that moment.

"Simple, Tommy! I thought I was going crazy with weird looks from providers and pharmacists, and I just needed to find out if there was a reason for their reactions," I answered him.

"So, is your argument that only Black people got negatively impacted by the Opioid Crisis?" He asked while sipping on his whiskey?

"Tommy, you are probably the only White person I can have this real race talk with without fear of it degenerating into an argument." I looked at him for a moment.

"Are you saying I'm not like all the other "White people" out there?" He asked with a smirk on his face. I laughed at his expression because I knew where this conversation was going.

"Tommy, you know what I mean!"

"Well, Jack, my stepfather is Black, and my two younger siblings are Bi-racial, and I've probably spent more time in the "hood" than you, which gave me a unique insight on Race."

"Spent more time in the "hood than me," so are you saying I'm not like all the other Black people you know?"

"Jack, I am glad those pain meds have not dulled your sense of humor; besides, this bar is amazing, as was the tour of Atlanta today." I laughed at his statement.

"Man, what can I say? We are a long way from Ridgewood – the worst neighborhood in Pleasantville, NJ." I reminded him of our worst childhood memory. We chatted for some time before we were interrupted by the waiter.

"Hello gentlemen, are you ready to Order? My name is Rory."

"Yes, this place has the best Cauliflower Crusted Pizza I've ever had; we will take two meat lovers," I said.

"Have you seen our drink menu?" Rory asked.

"Tommy, you are in my town, so please allow me. Since my "boy" over here is of Irish Descent, please give us two Irish Mules. Tommy, it's a vodka and ginger beer drink and a great way to start the evening." I felt lively after such a long time. I felt I was in my own buzz.

"And your choice for Cigars?"

"Do you have Good Trouble?"

"Yes, we do; it is a fine Cigar, and would you like a V-Cut?"

"Of course, Rory, thank you so much." We finally completed our full order.

"A V-CUT?" Tommy laughed, "you still **Boogie** as ever!" Tommy laughed!

"Don't hate, emulate!" I laughed too.

"Now, to answer your question, Tommy: I believe White people were terribly impacted by this Opioid Crisis, and this is supported by data. For example, Institutional Racism prevented African Americans from getting opioids and allowed it more easily and heavily for White people. Who then got addicted to the drugs, and with that, came the destruction of lives, families, and the current Opioid Crisis."

"Jack, you know my history. I have a chronic illness, got hooked on drugs, and at times did not have a roof over my head: Nobody gave a damn about me! Now, you tell me that Institutional Racism was the reason I gained greater access to opioids because doctors thought my skin was thinner than yours makes me angry as well. It took me years to "dig" out of that whole and turn my life around; maybe that is the reason I'm studying to become a priest? This way, I can help this population because the damage done by this Opioid crisis is still ongoing." Tommy made sense.

"Tommy, we were always brothers. Damn, your mom taught me how to eat apple sauce on pork chops?" We both laughed, remembering the good old days.

"Now we are brothers in a different way as our chronic illness makes us Brothers in Pain!"

"**Brothers in Pain**? I like that, Jack, because only someone going through the struggle of loss could understand the struggle; this makes us **Brothers in Pain**!" Now Tommy was in his own buzz.

"Oh, does that title work for women?" I asked.

"How about *Pain United*?"

"Give me some time; I will figure it out." We both laughed hysterically at our lamest joke, but our laughter was interrupted by the waiter who had brought our cigars.

"Gentlemen, here are your Cigars, would you like a light?"

"Yes, thank you," we replied while catching our breaths from the laughter.

"Your drinks will be right up," Rory informed.

"I really love this Cigar, Jack, and this place is very homey and diverse. It looks like a Rainbow Coalition here...I bet you spend hours here?"

"Yes, and as for the Cigar, I know the people who created the *Good Trouble Cigar*: **The ATL Cigar Company!**

It's an interesting story. Husband and wife Leroy and Janelle Lamar, along with Peter Gross, wanted to create a product that brought people together, given the strong divisions in our country. Years ago, they started with a Hot Dog stand, and now they sell some of the best cigars in Atlanta. The company's leadership is very diverse: The President of the company – Leroy, is a "Brotha" while the Marketing Guru - Janelle, is an Asian American; Peter, their Products guy, is White and used to play basketball with Seth Curry as a student at Davidson. So together, they produce a cigar that people from all three of these cultures would enjoy."

I just poured out all the little information I knew of my favorite place, maybe because it excited me to know that my friend loved this place as much as I did. We were then served our drinks. "Thank you for our drinks, Rory; how about a toast, Tommy?" I said while handing Tommy his drink.

"How about making it to 53?" Tommy added.

"Sounds good to me." We both then had our finest drinks as we further discussed the Opioid Crisis.

"Seriously, the Opioid Crisis has hurt both of our communities; the data was clear on that point as well. As for being a Chronic Pain patient, I don't think I've really looked at how it has impacted my Mental Health. I spend so much time coming up with systems to improve my body that I never thought about my mind, which is why Monique wants me to see a therapist." I finally discussed it with him. It was the first time I told someone – other than Monique -- about my need for therapy.

"So why don't you? After all, Mental Health is your business. Do you think it makes you weak or anything like that? Right?" he asked me.

"Of course, not Tommy; you know how we were raised; Mental Health was never talked about. I guess it's just hard for me to open up to someone I don't know, especially given how angry I am about what happened." I said while my fingers fiddled with the cocktail glass and smoking a cigar.

"I get your Anger, Jack. Some people very close to me did not accept me when I told them I was gay. I did not feel welcomed at Church anymore, and that was something I never got over." He was looking into my eyes".

"See the therapist, Jack; maybe she can help with the Anger you have over your loss." He said just like a friend would say.

"Tommy, you know how hard I worked, the countless hours and years of study to get here – where I can enjoy a cigar in a place like this. That accident could have happened to anybody, and it makes me feel like I don't have control of anything."

"Well, that is correct, Jack. God controls everything, and we are along for the ride, and we have our plans where God has its own. Think about the Book of Job; he never gave up and was rewarded in the end." He reminded me of another childhood memory.

"Well, Tommy, the story of Job always reminded me of the sitcom **Good Times**, honestly. The Evans family had five years of Temporary Layoffs and Scratching and Surviving; and only five minutes of Good Times in the end when folks got good jobs and college admission. Funny."

"That was funny as hell, Jack! I've never heard that analogy before, but it's on point. OK, then maybe God is testing your faith. You were always very analytical as a kid, always had a plan; maybe use this season in your life to work on your faith."

"So, work on my faith? Uhm, time to create a plan for that?" I asked innocently with a smirk on my face. Tommy laughed.

"Don't be a Smartass! You must have faith that you will get well, and it will happen – trust in God!"

"Tommy, I guess that is why you are becoming a Priest." I laughed.

"Thank you! Maybe the Therapist can help me on my faith journey as well?"

"It can't hurt; besides, I can help as I'm only a phone call away," he said.

"Yes, you are, and let's not wait so long to see each other again; I forgot how much fun it is having you around." I was genuinely glad to meet Tommy.

"Would you like another drink?" We heard Rory asking us.

"Can you give us two Uncle Nearest, one ice cube each?" I ordered again.

"Listen to you, "one ice cube each," Tommy mockingly mimicked.

"If the gang from Ridgewood could see you now...... My lord, they'll be shocked!" Tommy could barely breathe because of his hysterical laughter.

"Thanks for taking me out, Jack; maybe it was God's plan that I miss my connection today."

"Damn straight, Tommy, as I probably would not have pulled the "trigger" on this mental health treatment. Oh, Tommy, don't pour Uncle Nearest over your cup of ice, you just ruined the drink...."

We both laugh as we listen to Jeff sing "Georgia on My Mind."

Chapter 13

I spend 10% of my time problem and 90% of my time on the so-lution. Any problem can be solved if you have the "right" team!

It was a nice getaway with Tommy. I missed him, and I did not know until I met him. After my meeting with him, I got back on my therapist search. I googled Dr. Feelings and saw that she was a licensed psychologist that was Board Certified in Clinical Health Psychology. She had been the director of the Atlanta Center for Behavioral Medicine in Atlanta, Georgia, since 1994. Dr. Feelings specialized in pain management and trauma, and her practice was dedicated to the evaluation and treatment of Acute and Chronic Pain.

Dr. Feelings treatment plans were goal-directed and problem-focused, with the goals of effectively managing the pain and leading a more productive life. In addition to treatment, she conducted psychological evaluations to assist with treatment planning and to assist in determining if the patient is an appropriate candidate, from a psychological standpoint, for medical procedures, such as surgery and spinal cord stimulation. She received her PhD in 1987 and was an African American.

It seemed like Dr. Feelings was tailored-made for someone with Chronic Pain. I felt Dr. Feelings would understand many of the complex issues which were associated with me as an African American that worked hard his whole life to have everything turned upside down due to circumstances beyond his control. It would take about six weeks, but I found myself finishing a cup of coffee while entering Dr. Feeling's Smyrna office.

I was very nervous for some reason as I took stock of her office. It looked more like a home than anything else, with the hardwood floors, African Art, and prints on the wall. I was welcomed by her. "It is a pleasure meeting you, Mr. Dunbar," she said as she shook my hand warmly.

She looked a bit like Mary Mcleod Bethune, an African American educator, and former head of Bethune Cookman College.

I was a little overwhelmed as I came into her office, but we sat down. She offered me coffee, and I agreed. I could feel my heart throbbing for absolutely no reason and my fingers trembling. I was trying to control my nervousness.

"So, where should we begin this from?" I finally made eye contact with her and asked about the procedure.

Working in the industry, I knew that the first session is more of a "deep dive" diagnostic for the Psychologist to obtain all the information she/he need to make a diagnosis. This session normally takes about an hour; my session with Dr. Feelings spent lasted for three hours that day.

"I am very proud of you, Mr. Dunbar. Very few patients make the changes you did to put their health first. That level of drive is inspiring, and you should take a moment to "breathe" and reflect on the positive changes that made you a healthier person." She tried to encourage me.

"If you are talking about the weight loss and body changes, none of that matters if pain prevents me from playing with my kids," I replied in a low voice while playing with my hands and avoiding eye contact.

"Ahh, so you prefer to spend your time focused on what you can't do instead of what you can do? Focusing on your problem and not on solutions," she said.

I looked at her, and she could sense my rage -- I replied angrily:

"Do you think I've been sitting on my ass watching "Springer" all day? I am a very process-oriented guy and have used those skills set to create **methods** that helped me:

- Lost 90lbs – I lost more than 20% of my body weight.

- Get my A1C to 5.2 – It was an 8.7 on my first ER visit.

- Turn all my body indicators, like Cholesterol, all green.

I did all of this in Pain, and my so-called medical experts did not deliver a pain-ending surgery. So, what happens now?"

I nearly yelled, trying to fight back the tears my tears.

"I've fought this pain for three years, and I am just so fucking tired. Even today, I did not take my morning pills so I could be lucid during this discussion. Which meant I drove her in rush hour traffic in pain, and my hands were shaking because of all the cars on the road. All I want is my life back. Can you help me with that, Dr. Feelings? Can you really help?"

She remained silent the entire time while writing in her notebook. It reminded me of a show which Monique, and I used to watch: "Monk" – a show about a Police Detective who sees his therapist daily – and Monk was always worried about what his therapist was writing in his files during their session. I always thought that was funny, but now I could feel his fear.

Talking to Dr. Feelings was like opening myself up so she could see the good, the bad, and the ugly. I was **NAKED** in a way I've never been with any other person in my life. Not even Monique had seen me this exposed and weak; maybe this was why I *pushed back so* hard about getting mental health treatment.

"Mr. Dunbar, do you understand how I help my chronic pain patients? She asked after some time.

"No, I do not, Dr. Feelings, please school me," I stated.

Here is what she told me:

"First, I help my patients accept the "New Reality" of their current

physical state. Many of you CEO/Alpha types have a hard time

accepting limitations due to physical incapacity. In other words,

you must learn to do less, so you can do more.

Then we spend time creating a team of provider-specialists tasked

with making you the healthiest version of yourself, given your

new limitations. These specialties include:

⇒ *Finances*	*Primary Medicine*
⇒ *Mobility Technology*	*Aquatic/Land Rehab*
⇒ *Pain Management*	*Alternative Medicine*
⇒ *Psychiatry*	

Lastly, I help my patients develop "methods" to improve their quality of life.

"So, are you ready to get to work, Mr. Dunbar?" she asked me after sharing her methods.

"Dr. Feelings, "I was raised to Work Hard, Be Smart with Money and to Never Give Up! – so yeah, I am ready!"

That day, Monique and I had a long discussion about my session over dinner.

"I think you found a winner."

Monique said while having a glass of red wine.

"Yes, I agree, and her solutions focus can only enhance my own Anger Focus method of achieving my goals," I said.

"You got lucky, honey; sometimes it can take years to "match" with a good therapist. I am just so proud that you finally took action on your Mental Health; too many Black Men in Chronic Pain fail to do so, and I've seen that lead to devastating consequences during my 25-year Psychiatric career." Monique stroked my head gently, and I felt at peace.

Chapter 14

FINANCES

There is nothing worse than putting your hand in your pocket to only feel your leg – I hate it when my money is funny!

Dr. Feelings and I then began meeting twice a month. We would begin with a general overview of what happened to me during the prior two weeks, then focus on one of her "help areas". Accepting my limitations was tough. I was in my late 40's, in reasonable shape, with two young kids, a wife, and a business that needed caretaking. Dr. Feelings unpacked all of it:

"Mr. Dunbar," I reviewed your medical records and can tell you that you are way too active for someone in your condition. You must be in constant pain and are making things far worse by not delegating work and home responsibilities.

How I replied? We seriously reduced operations at work, so there is less money being generated.

"Don't you have a legal case pending?"

Yes, in fact, I just had my deposition this week, so hopefully, we can get some type of settlement from my car insurance company State Farm.

"Tell me about the deposition?"

Peter, my lawyer told me it would be at his office and that two lawyers, one from Snake 1 -- my insurance company and Snake 2 -- the driver's insurer would be present. I told him that I would go off meds during the deposition so I could have a clear head.

Peter said, it would only take a few hours, but I was stuck in that office for the whole eight-hour day.

That morning, I knew that the lawyers would be "sizing me up" and trying to "trip me up" to gauge if they would settle, and if so, how much they would give. I selected my clothes as if I was going to trial:

- My hair cut was "High and Tight" and clean shaven.
- Basic black shoes, shines to perfection by my son.
- The clothes:
  - Black Jeans
  - White buttoned-down shirt -- no tie
  - Dark blue checkered sports coat

They started with Monique -- a Psychiatrist on the shortlist of many lawyers in town due to her times spent as an expert witness. Monique is extremely likable and very smart; she had those lawyers eating out of her hands.

Then the two lawyers started in on me. My story was simple: Family man married for almost 20 years, with a thriving business, gets cut down in his prime and now is suffering the permanent effects of this tragedy. My story flowed like a well-rehearsed pitch whose objective was to close a big deal. I think the reason it went over so well was that it was the truth. They saw me as a "Honest Plaintiff", which meant they would write a check. The question then became: How big should the check be?"

That was when they presented evidence of my past injuries to limit the size of the check:

"Is it not true that you had back issues in the past Mr. Dunbar?" For instances you fell off your bike during a triathlon in 2009 and did rehab for almost a year."

"That is true, but I overcame that injury. In fact, in 2013 my wife and I celebrated our 10th year anniversary with a walking tour though Italy, and we walked for miles every day. Peter, then showed them a picture of my running up the "Leaning

- 135 -

Tower of Pizazz and jumping from steps in the Coliseum yelling

"I AM SPARTACUS"!

I also ran the July 2014 Peachtree Road Race with my wife, walked the 3 miles back to our car, then had a Barbecue for me friend where I did all the cooking. Does that sound like someone with a Back Injury? Damn, I can barely walk down the street assisted with two canes.

"How about this injury in 2008, I have the doctor's note where you state your back "went out" while you were in your home?"

"What are you talking about I stated, I don't remember a back injury, can I please read the doctor's medical record? *"Patient Jackson Dunbar was having sex with his wife where they attempted to have sex in every room of their home."*

I laughed my butt off, as did the female lawyer and stenographer. Peter had a big ass smile on his face as well. I then stated, "at least you know why my wife married me! More laughs! I knew how to handle business, something my injury prevents me from doing today."

We went back and forth, each time I gave a "reasonable" explanation for everything. I was in so much pain that I began to sweat and then gave probably one of the best closing arguments of my life:

- I used to be a Man, in every way possible.

- Now I can't play with my kids.

- Sex with my wife is an impossibility.

- My prospects to make money have eroded.

- Constant unabating pain is my reality.

- A big check was needed as my injuries were permanent.

My lawyer had a big smile on his face when we finished and stated, "You should be working for me!"

"Well Mr. Dunbar, do you think they will settle with you soon asked Dr. Feelings"?

"No! My best friend Howard did well for himself in the insurance business. He stated that the insurance companies would delay payment as long as possible. It's about the time value of money: Money is worth more now, than in the future, because it can be immediately invested. In essence, the longer they can hold onto my money, the longer they can invest it and make more money from it. I would be lucky to get a check in two years from **Snake 1**, but **Snake 2** -- the driver's insurer – had already settled.

"What will you do until then Mr. Dunbar?"

"Live off investment income and savings. When I get the check, the plan is to make the money work for my family:

- Pay off all credit debt.

- Eliminate any car loans.

- Buy my wife something nice

- Build a three-to-six-month emergency fund

- Invest the remainder in the top five ETFs on the stock market, that also pay dividends.

"How would you do that Mr. Dunbar; don't you need a financial advisor and what is an ETF"?

"An ETF, or exchange-traded fund, is an investment security that combines some of the attributes of stocks and <u>mutual funds</u>. Like stocks, ETFs trade intra-day on an exchange. Like with mutual funds, many ETFs seek to track the performance of a benchmark index, such as the <u>S&P 500</u>.

Because ETFs are <u>passively managed</u>, the operational costs are extremely low compared to actively managed portfolios. It's common for an ETF expense ratio to be lower than 0.10%, which is just $10 annually for every $10,000 of investments. Financial Planners charge around two to four percent of the portfolio's value. So, if the value of your portfolio is 10,000, then the fee charged could go up to $400 per year."

"Are you also a Financial Planner, I know you have a Law Degree and MBA?"

"No, I am not a financial planner, and you don't have to be one to buy ETFs and Stocks – it is sort of a hobby. The best way to start:

- Set up a Brokerage account with Merrill Edge, Fidelity.com, etc.

- Google the names for the top ETFs during the last year, that also pays dividends. I selected these Commodity-Based positions because the cost of things life food and energy keep going up, which means the value of Commodity-Based ETF should go up:

  o **_COM_**: _The Direxion Auspice Broad Commodity Strategy ETF_ allows investors to take advantage of rising commodity prices, in addition to mitigate risk by going flat (cash) when individual commodities are experiencing downward trends. It seeks to potentially provide commodity investment returns with lower risk characteristics than long-only commodity strategies. It's one-year return was 28% and it pays quarterly dividends of $3.01

- o **FTGC**: _The First Trust Global Tactical Commodity Strategy Fund_ is an actively managed exchange-traded fund that seeks total return and a relatively stable risk profile while providing investors with commodity exposure. It's one-year return was 27% and pays a quarterly dividend of $1.66 per share.

- o **BCD**: _Aberdeen Standard Bloomberg All Commodity Longer Dated Strategy K-1 Free ETF_ The fund invests in exchange-traded commodity futures contracts through a wholly owned subsidiary of the fund organized under the laws of the Cayman Islands. It's one-year return is 31% and pays a yearly dividend of $2.55.

- Divide the money between the positions and review every three months.

Lastly, as I "stepped away" from WellMed/Atlanta to focus on my health; and so, am living on savings; I would use the money made from the interests/dividends in my positions to pay for my ongoing medical costs and family expenses".

"It sounds like you have a sound financial plan Mr. Dunbar." Could a person with limited experience complete these investments?"

"I do not see why not? This strategy assumes that someone is getting a "bulk" some of cash, perhaps from a settlement; that they have paid off credit cards and built an emergency fund. Once that is done, then it becomes simple to invest.

Oh, almost forgot, I found other people interested in investing and we formed a blog where we share investing ideas. I've received some great leads investing this way and it gives me an opportunity to have other people give me insight on my "picks".

"Well, I see that you have your finances "buttoned" up; can we talk about your two canes, have you ever thought about using a scooter?"

"Monique and my mom suggested that I use a scooter for the year. The other day, my daughter drew a picture of our family. There was the house, dog, and family members. What broke me was that I was way in the back, and the three of them were walking in front of me. My daughter was young when I got hurt, so she only knows me as sick. My son remembers when I used to be strong when we used to play and exercise together; for this reason, my accident has been hard on Miles".

"Well, if you used a scooter, Mr. Dunbar, then you would be able to keep up with your family with minimal pain as there would be no pressure on your joints".

"I will pray on it, Dr. Feelings, but I feel I am giving up on using the device."

"Nonsense Mr. Dunbar, you have to decide between your ego and your pain, and I will be curious to see where you land."

Chapter 15

Mobility Technology is a Game Changer for those with Chronic Pain and life on a scooter is a "Different World."

I participated in one of the beloved ministries of my church; one of my team members was an elder of the Church. Her name was Linda, and she also rode a mobility scooter and asked me if I ever thought of doing so? I told her that my mother had my great uncle's old scooter and offered it to me as a gift, which I declined.

Linda then stated that *"Pride and Ego should not be part of my decision-making process."*

My church also created a "Handicapped Seating" at the front of the pews. The normal pews are very hard and, in my case, cause nerve irritation and low back pain when I sit too long. Monique asked me why I did not use the "seating," and I told her I was not ready and felt embarrassed as everyone that did was about twice my age. Linda would ask me about scooters every time she saw me. I even tried to avoid her during one service.

One night at our night ministry, Linda gave me an "Enabling Life" magazine with scores of scooters for purchase. I thanked her and thought about the scooter my mother had offered me months ago. It belonged to my great uncle, who was now deceased, but she said the scooter was in great condition as it was never used.

The following week, my family visited Clearwater Beach for our summer vacation. It was a cheap trip, we had good weather, and the water was very calm – perfect for swimming. As we walked down the beach, we noticed several mobility scooter rentals. I rented a scooter, and it was so big that I could carry our ice chest, book bags, towels, and canes.

The scooter was GREAT! I was able to keep up with my family, carry most of the things we needed for the day, and I was not thinking about my pain all day. By 6 pm, I was happy and playing with my family instead of laying down in sheer agony like in previous vacations when attempting to walk with my canes. The scooter was able to travel a long distance, go up hills, and take away all the "pounding on my spine" that occurs when I am trying to be active. I talked to Monique, and we decided to accept my mom's offer of the scooter.

We stopped at my mother's on the way home, who showed me the chair, and it was a perfect fit. It was a *Golden Companion Three-Wheel Mobility Scooter* that offered more leg and foot room with a wider front deck. It was easy to disassemble and had a large, comfortable padded seat. Whoever designed it knew what they were doing as the seat was very comfortable and had lots of lumbar support.

Mom left me alone with the scooter and told me to remember:

"Suffering produces Perseverance, Perseverance produces

Character and Hope, and we must keep always Hope alive."

(Romans 5: 3-5)

Then I thought about my great Uncle Charlie. He was called Papa Bear as he was 6ft 3, weight about 280, and looked like a lumberjack. He was a veteran of the Korean War, surviving "Pork Chop Hill." He had a 10-inch scar that went down his stomach, and as a kid, he would often tell us the story of how he got that scar:

"We were fighting for our lives those days. Our superior weaponry met nothing against the hordes of soldiers of the enemy. The enemy was composed of well-armed Korean soldiers backed up by millions of Chinese soldiers; some even fought barefoot. We all thought the same thing, "Where was our DAMN air support!

*Our ammo ran out; with bayonets in hand, it was man against man, **then man against ten men**. I was stabbed but kept fighting because not doing so met certain death! I bled on the field for a day, maybe more, and it was freezing! We were later rescued, and this scar is a constant reminder that God would always be with me, as I should have died that* day!"

I pulled the scooter out of the garage, changed the batteries with Miles's help, and rode around the neighborhood thinking and thanking my Uncle Charlie. This was the scooter of a man that survived one of the bloodiest battles in US Military history. He did not give up, and I will follow that example. I would use this scooter, this technology, to help me with my family and business. I would see Linda a few days later at church, and she said, *"I am glad that you decided to use the scooter, "Welcome to a New World."*

I did not know what Linda meant until the next day when a man farted in my face at the Farmers' Market. Then, I had my first pitch on the scooter, and it was a failure! Now I know how Women feel when Men are looking at them instead of listening to their words.

Everyone from the Front Office staff to the decision-maker stared at the scooter. My scooter became the elephant in the room, and it was unnerving. We did not get the contract, and I found myself wondering how I could perform my job as our company's sales resource if people were going to impart my disability onto my company's ability to do its job.

Also, my alma mater – Tulane Law – had an alumni meet & greet at a local law firm near the High Museum in Midtown Atlanta. I would have to go off meds to be lucid during the event, which meant I would have to use my scooter. I went to the parking lot and could not find any handicapped parking. The guard told me to drive up to the upper level of the parking lot to gain entry to the elevator that would take me to the Law Firm hosting the party. I parked, got my scooter, and could not go to the elevator because I had to walk down the steps. I could not believe there was no ramp to the elevator. Several lawyers came out and could not believe it either. I called security and had to wait for 20 minutes before getting assistance.

I tuck a deep breath as the elevator's door opened and prayed. I turned to the left, got my name sticker, turned around, and saw a bunch of suits staring at me. I told myself, "I could do this," and started "shaking hands and kissing babies."

It was fun meeting some of my old classmates, and the "Marketeer" inside of me began to segment the group:

- Younger attorneys had little problem networking with me.

- African American attorneys of all ages spoke with me as well.

- The over 55 clubs, the decision-makers, were polite but kept their distance.

I hugged Monique when arriving home and told her it was going to take time to become accustomed to this "New World!"

"How do you feel now about using the scooter, Mr. Dunbar?"

"It has been a real adjustment Dr. Feelings. There are so many buildings in this town with no wheelchair access, and I've had people "fart" in my face at the grocery store. The hardest thing is trying to "close deals" while in the scooter."

"Why is that Mr. Dunbar?"

"I am 6'1 and weigh about 250lbs. As a Black Man, I've always had to hold myself back in negotiations and when dealing with people so they would not be afraid of me. Now, I find that people try to take advantage of me or even talk down to me. I don't want to say, "they think I am a pushover," but it feels like I must be more assertive in the chair?"

"Lastly, it has been a total adjustment for my family. We were in Savanah, and I could not get into many of the stores in the historic district because they were non-handicap accessible. We wanted to ride on street cars, and they were not accessible – It became very frustrating! Then we were in one establishment that had a lift for folks with mobility needs, and the thing broke down while I was using it. It took them almost 30 minutes to get me out of there."

"Mr. Dunbar, what did that teach you?"

That I need to create a **Mobility Action Plan** when traveling to another city, elements of the plan could include:

- See if the city is Wheelchair Accessible; I found numerous "disabled travel sites on Google like:

  www.wheelchairtraveling.com

  Started by Ashley Lyn Olson, who has been paralyzed since age 14, it is an online community for travelers with disabilities. Once on the site, you can research cities across the U.S, as well as countries around the globe.

- Research the costs of renting Wheelchair Accessible Vans or Taxis in a city.
  - Be prepared for sticker shock when you get prices for these vehicles. I've paid rates as high as $100 dollars for a Wheelchair Accessible Van, as well as $200 dollars a day, plus a three 3-day minimum to rent a Wheelchair Accessible Van to attend a two-day funeral.
  - Why did I pay? There are few providers that offer this service in cities around the country. Further, LIFT and UBER have a very LIMITED

Wheelchair Accessible Van "Footprint" – currently beta-testing in Boston, London, Chicago, Los Angeles, New York, Philadelphia, San Francisco, Toronto, and Washington DC.

- o Since there is a limited supply of Wheelchair Accessible "service" vehicles, the few providers that offer the service charge **MUCH** higher prices than a normal taxi or Van Rental.

- Check the costs of renting a scooter in a destination city if you do not want to bring your own.

- Check hotels for Disabled Friendly rooms, which tend to be bigger and in short supply.

- Check Assistance Required when booking a flight. This way, you can ride your scooter to the gate, have it checked when you board, and then it is returned to you at the gate when you arrive at your destination.

"Excellent, Mr. Dunbar. You learned from your negative experience in Savannah and adopted new methods to limit that type of exposure again. And regarding closing "deals" in the "chair," -- My advice is to be yourself. Let that confidence be seen whether or not you are in the "chair." As for people who may not do business with you because of seeing you in the chair – their loss! I ask you; would you do business with a firm that felt uncomfortable working with African Americans?"

"NO!! I would not!"

"In that case, Mr. Dunbar, "**Same Strokes for Different Folks**."

I laughed my ass off while "rolling" out of Dr. Feelings' office.

Dr. Feelings was correct!!

Chapter 16

Pain Medicine

All you really need is hope, strength, and will: hope it will change, strength to hold on until it does, and the will to make the necessary changes to improve your quality of life.

I sat in Dr. Pain-Free's office looking outside of the window, thinking almost four years and I am still not "fixed."

"Mr. Dunbar, you have had several "injections," with each giving you less relief; so, I feel that we should explore a Radiofrequency Ablation:

- Dr. "Pain-Free" would burn the area around the nerves granting pain relief, and cost roughly $4500.

- **Promised**: Pain relief for up to 12 months.

- **My results**: Pain score dropped from 9 to 4 for six weeks, then full acute pain returned.

When I returned for my next appointment, Dr. Pain-Free stated she wanted to decrease my pain medications. Yelling, I was barely hanging on with what I was one now; Monique urged me to listen to Dr. Pain-Free" and respect her process.

I stated, "at what costs? I can barely function on these medications, and now she wanted to cut them even more! Has anyone explored the use of lower dose "opioids" for Pain Management?" Monique stated, "The issue is that your body would get used to the dosage and require more, leading to addition – A path neither Dr. Pain-Free nor I want for you."

Here is your medication plan:

- You stop taking Tramadol
- We put you on Low Dose Naltrexone
  - Naltrexone, in low doses of up to 4.5mg, has been shown to reduce pain.
- Start you on Tizanidine
- Increase Gabapentin
- Use Ibuprofen – up to 800mg, 3x a day.

"Baby, respect the process," said Monique, "and let's give this new plan a shot. Low Dose Naltrexone, used for pain, is experimental; thus, your insurance would not cover the price." Thankfully, Emory filled the medications using "select pharmacies" that charged lower rates for the medication. I still wondered if Low Dose Naltrexone would be as good as Tramadol or Suboxone– only time would tell?

Dr. Pain-Free also discussed:

The Spinal Stimulator Implant:

- A Pacemaker" for the spine would be "hardwired to my spine, possessing wires protruding from my body and attaching to a device on my hip. This device would trick my brain into thinking it was not in pain and cost $30,000 to 50,000.

- *They promised*: Pain Relief for years.

- *Research Found*: Up to three months recovery time and has a failure rate of 25% to 30%

I was informed that the Stimulator would be better than a Fusion, as I could "get off" many of the medications that cause mental "fog" and possible organ damage. The average age of patients who have this procedure was 65 years old, so it was the procedure of last resort.

My head was spinning with all this information. My wife was present and did an excellent job talking me through all the pros and cons. Lastly, stated by Dr. "Pain-Free", we would need to complete a **Spinal Stimulator Trial** to see if the procedure would even work on your body:

- Small temporary "leads" or wires would be placed in my lower back using a small needle.
- The "leads" would be attached to an external battery taped to my body.
- No showers or swimming was allowed during the trial.

This outpatient procedure took about an hour. The device itself was weird: I had a wire sticking out of my body; and was told it was an open wound, so I had to stay stationary. Bandages wrapped the entire area, and that was reinforced with tape. I went hope, but it was very uncomfortable to lay down as the stimulator was hanging out of my body. To get an accurate baseline, I took fewer doses of my medication. That was a very long night as I could not sleep as the stimulator was uncomfortable. I was very stiff the next morning and in a lot of pain due to the surgery itself. I had my t-shirt off and was brushing my teeth when my daughter began screaming and crying. She yelled, "Daddy is hurt and bleeding."

Monique came running into the bedroom and saw that the bandages were soaked with blood due to the open hole caused by the wire. The red soaked bandage looked like a "crime scene," but I lied to my daughter and told her it was no big deal. I then went back to the hospital to have the bandage changed.

I woke up the next day and felt nothing. No numbness and no pain. I felt pretty damn good. I did extra activities around the house and office at the kids' school, just trying to give this technology a workout. When the trial was over, I told Dr. Feelings that I thought everything went well. My wife stated my mood had changed as well. I looked very happy and had not brooded at all during the trial. I asked if the device could remain until after Christmas. My wife and Dr. Feelings said that would not be prudent as I was still leaking through the open wound, and that could cause an infection.

The permanent procedure would take over three hours and might require a hospital stay. Also, I would need to remain, albeit stationary, for a month, so the device to get stabilized within my body. Lastly, the recovery time could take up to four months. We have no family in Atlanta and given the kid'' school activities and work obligations, it made sense to put the procedure off until the summer.

At that time, my mother could come up and help during the summer as I healed from the operations. Also, the irony of all this just hit me:

- The use of the stimulator met years of procedures for the rest of my life as the device would need continued maintenance, battery changes, and lots of pain due to the operations.

- Not using the stimulator meant I would remain in my current position: Dependent on mind-numbing medications that destroy my quality of life, physical therapy that can't get rid of scar tissue, and the probable need for other surgeries – like Fusions–- as I grow older, and my symptoms got worse.

Two weeks later, I thought about these outcomes as I completed my 30 laps in the pool. I was in a hurry as I had to pick up the kids from school; when I mistakenly twisted my body to the left, and my lower body went limp.

A couple of guys got me off the floor, and the feeling in my lower body returned. I went to the Emergency Room, and their scans found instability in my spine. This was very bad news because it meant that I could not have the Spinal Stimulator Implant as that procedure requires a stable spine.

Dr. Feelings, "God must be a comedian, "as I laughed during my session.

"How are your spirits, Mr. Dunbar?" Are you still swimming and taking care of yourself?"

The only place where there is no pain is the pool, so yes, I spend five days a week there. I had so many hopes and dreams, and it was all taken away by a freak accident that could have happened to anyone.

"Mr. Dunbar" let's focus on what we can do to improve your quality of life. How is your diet coming?"

"I don't know why, but it is harder to lose weight. Ever since my last medication change, for every two pounds I lose, I gain one. In fact, I seem to have fluid retention, which causes weight gain, even while eating the right foods. Swimming and my time in the YMCA sauna have become a necessity, as that is the only thing that prevents fluid retention".

"Mr. Dunbar, the issue may be the recent increase in dosage of Gabapentin – a drug known for weight gain. I want you to visit your Primary Care doctor – and ask if he has any suggestions to continue your weight loss. The best way to manage your pain is to:

- Continue your weight loss which will reduce pressure on your lower back.
- Maintain a "zero impact" exercise program–- like swimming – which has no pressure on the joints.
- Remove anti-inflammatory food from your diet as this will decrease the amount of pain in your body and include:
  o White bread and pastries
  o Fried Food
  o Soda
  o Red and Processed Meats

"An excellent book on the subject is "Eat to Live."

I don't know about giving up "Steak," but at this point, I am

willing to do anything.

Chapter 17

Primary Care

"I would pay $2 Million Dollars for the ability to "Pee" without it hurting. I spent my whole life making a lot of money and would give it all up for one healthy day" –
Hymon Roth -- The Godfather Part II

I've been "stuck" around 260lbs for over a year, and I need to lose another 30lbs Dr. PCP. I tried cutting carbs the other day, almost passed out at my local Panera, and then could not remember where to park the car. Monique thought I was on a lot of medications, so it might be prudent to ask my primary care physician – Dr. PCP, for help.

"Mr. Dunbar, you not only dropped 90lbs but also kept the weight off during the years you've been treated. Your body may be used to your current eating plan and so has plateaued. I think it is time to mix things up: Have you ever heard about Emory's Bariatric Center?"

"Yes, sort of, as I see their offices across the hall on my way to the elevator."

"The Bariatric Center uses Surgical and Nonsurgical options to help people lose weight and maintain weight loss. They have a multidisciplinary team that includes bariatric surgeons, a medical bariatrician, dietitians, and consulting psychologists. The strength of the weight loss program lies in the individualized approach and ongoing support, including medical monitoring, wellness coaching, nutrition counseling, and support group meetings."

"That sounds like a plan, Dr. PCP; I will "roll" over there and get signed up."

It took about three weeks to get an appointment. I met Dr. WW, and he really impressed me with his knowledge of body chemistry. He went through my medical records and stated I was on two medications that cause water retention and weight gain, but he could not change the dosage as it would disrupt my pain protocol. The worst, **Gabapentin** is a drug he suggests all new Bariatric patients stop because it is HARD to lose weight on that medication.

He then took my weight on some fancy NASA-looking scale which also took my BMI – Body Mass Index. Measurements of my body were then taken to get a baseline, and then I asked about the surgical options. Dr. WW laughed because my BMI was not high enough for any of the surgical options. "God is a Comedian," I stated. So back when I was 350lb, I would have been a candidate for surgery, but now that I've lost 90lbs, I am on my own?

He stated that their non-Surgical options called "**YOUR WEIGH**" would be more appropriate for someone with my BMI; the program included:

Program Enrollment and Baseline Evaluation:

- Prior to beginning the program, you would undergo a battery of metabolic and blood tests and meet with one of our dietitians to complete a nutritional and lifestyle assessment. Our bariatrician is a medical doctor who specializes in the field of bariatrics. He will meet with you to complete a history and physical assessment and review your test results.

Weekly lifestyle education groups:

- They offer social support, behavior modification tools, instruction in increasing physical activity and incorporating good nutrition into your daily lives, and suggestions for adhering to the program.

Weekly clinic visits will include:

- The registration and payment for the product for those who do not pay in full before beginning the program at our front desk.

NOTE: Product orders will be distributed after payment if on the weekly payment plan.

Weight, vital signs, waist circumference taken by our medical assistants -Reassessment with our bariatrician approximately every four weeks (Reassessment with our

clinical dietitian approximately every four weeks).

MEAL PLANS:

- *Full Meal Replacement Option*: Your product intake will be

  5 (or 6, at the physician's discretion) OPTIFAST® meal

  replacements per day. Due to the very low-calorie intake on

  this meal plan, you will be monitored more frequently by our

  physician and will have blood drawn approximately every

  other week.

- *Partial Meal Replacement Option*: Your product intake will

  be limited to three (3) OPTIFAST® meal replacements of

  your choice per day, plus the healthy food choices you

  incorporate into your diet based on the educational portion of

  your program and individual meetings with our dietitians.

- *No Meal Replacement Option*: You will follow the intake

  guidelines discussed during the educational portion of your

program and individual meetings with our dietitians. Please see our "Partial- and No- Meal Replacement Meal Plan."

The costs for the "Full Meal" replacement were $1,375 dollars for the program and $1,249.50 for the food, totaling $2,624.50. I did the math, and it was cheaper than having another surgery; I just hoped the food tasted good. "I told him he had me at "Hello Mr. Dunbar." The nutrition program would take six months, and I hoped for the best, Dr. Feelings."

"So, is this Bariatric plan covered under your insurance, Mr. Dunbar?"

"No, I had to pay out of pocket as this was a new experimental program. I did check with my health insurance providers, and they did cover the use of a Nutritionist. My insurance sponsors a similar "Weight Loss" program, but they did not have an opening for three months."

"Which plan did you select, Mr. Dunbar.?"

I selected the "Partial Meal" plan, that's three (3) meal replacements a day: Two Shakes and One Protein Bar. I would "swap out" three small meals from my "Plug and Chuck" Meal Plan for a combined five (5) meals."

"How does it taste, Mr. Dunbar?"

"It's good! I was presently surprised, and the replacement meals are portable. I eat the Protein Bar after swimming while at the pool or drink a shake – which is premade – while I am at my doctor's. I had to change my eating plan:

I also had to cut my calories a bit to offset the water retention from Gabapentin. This meant I had to also reduce my exercise and swim times:

My current S.M.A.R.T Goals and the best way to change them:

- **Specific**: I needed to lose another 30lbs, maintain my A1C to under 6.0, keep my Blood Pressure to under 120/80 and keep all other indicators green.

- **Measurable**: I would record my measurements and weight daily.

- **Attainable**: My swim plan needed to change:

  - Decrease Swim Time to 800 meters -- 32 laps back and forth – in Wade Walker YMCA's 25-meter pool. Wade Walker is a YMCA in Stone Mountain – It is a very diverse membership consisting of People of Color from across America, Europe, Asia, and Africa. It also has the best pool in Atlanta, in my opinion.

  - Maintain 30 Minutes in Sauna/Whirlpool – My medications make me retain water; thus, being in the Sauna helps me eliminate that water by sweating heavily.

  - Decrease swim time to three days a week: Swimming was my only cardio, and I burned at least 300 calories per session.

- **Relevant** – Dr. WW had to approve my new Plug and Chuck Plan:

Dr. WW approved my eating plan and cautioned me about building too much muscle. The issue was that muscle weighed more than fat, which would put more pressure on my back.

"Well, Mr. Dunbar, I bet your wife is happy that you are getting in shape? How often are you having sex"?

That question hit me like a punch from Mike Tyson! They call it "Loss of Consortium." It means that there has been a disruption of a married couple's quality of life due to sickness or death. Stated another way, I was in so much pain that getting an erection was nigh impossible. Further, if by some miracle I did get an erection, once the pounding associated with sex began, the erection ceased due to pain.

"Are you going to answer my question, Mr. Dunbar?"

Not able to look Dr. Feelings in the eye, I told her about my

Erectile Dysfunction. We try to have sex, but it just does not

happen, and now, we stop trying due to disappointment. It is

funny; I got more sex when weighing 350lbs than now at my

current weight of 265. Maybe my wife preferred me "Large and

in Charge"!

"Laughing so hard she choked on tea – Mr. Dunbar, I doubt that

is the case, though I would be frustrated as hell too. Have you

tried Viagra or Cialis?"

"Viagra. My PCP put me on the medication; it costs a fortune

and is not working."

"Let me recommend a Urology team – Midtown Urology: These

urologists specialize in the diagnosis and treatment of diseases of

the urinary track. In essence, Mr. Dunbar, they may have a bet-

ter solution to solve your ED."

"Thank you, Dr. Feelings. I got married later in life, something

my father always suggested. He would tell my brother and me to

"Travel the World" and discover "tools" that you can put in a "toolbox"; so that when you get married, you are able to "BUILD" a house with your wife.

"Laughing, does that mean what I think it does, Mr. Dunbar?"

Yes, while laughing, it does! I hope these guys can help me use my "MAIN" tool again?!

"Oh, Mr. Dunbar, stop, and I will see you next time, still laughing."

Chapter 18

UROLOGY

"If it Ain't Right in the bedroom, then it Ain't Right!"
My Dad

A lot of people must have "Dick" problems, I thought, pulling into the Midtown Urology offices. It took almost two months to get this appointment, and I was hopeful that the providers could fix my Erectile Dysfunction. I loved the décor in the office; African American Art was nicely placed, as well as the numerous awards the providers had received over the years. The staff put with Dr. ED, as Dr. URO -- the Chief Partner – was out of town. Dr. URO was a world-renowned Urologist with medical degrees from Duke and Emory. I did not know much about Dr. ED but was just glad to have an appointment.

After getting my vitals, I was placed in a waiting room and just trying to take everything in when I heard, "Good Morning Mr., Dunbar; I am Dr. ED."

My mouth dropped because Dr. ED was a Woman! I never considered that the person who would be "grabbing my dick" and telling me to cough would be some woman other than my wife. My mind was fixated on her well-groomed nails on my balls when Dr. ED stated, "Please tell me why you are here?"

I was being sexist. Crap! my wife is a doctor. Steeling my nerve, I gave her my history as if we were two strangers at a warm campfire.

"Can you get and or maintain an erection?"

"No, it is very hard to get an erection, then when it occurs, I am unable to maintain it once the "pounding" associated with sex starts. I get "soft" as soon as the pain starts, which then leads to the lower left side of my body getting numb."

"Have you tried Cialis, as some of my patients prefer it over Viagra?"

"No, and at this point, I am open to anything."

"Let's start you out at a 5mg a day dosage, but first, I need to get a urine sample and perform a rectal exam."

"Ohh, no problem," I lied and said, "I normally have to buy someone dinner before they ask me to take off my pants."

Dr. ED looked at me, and I could tell that "Humor" was my way of dealing with awkward situations."

Putting on gloves, she said, "Mr. Dunbar, are you able to stand as I was sitting on my scooter?"

"Sure," as I stood totally bare, Dr. ED felt around my gentiles then stated,

"Everything feels good here; please bend over for the prostrate exam."

O boy, I bent over, feeling her fingers in my rectum, and stated, "It's been a long time since someone other than my wife has been around this part of my body."

"That was funny, Mr. Dunbar; your prostate is good. Now, let's talk about your options moving forward. We will start with 5mg daily doses, which should take the same time every day. Please let us know its effectiveness at your next appointment. We can increase the dosage up to 20 mg, which is the maximum recommended daily dosage."

"Sometimes, I do not feel anything in my groin area. Is this a sign my nerve damage could be impacting that area?"

"Perhaps, but we do have several solutions if either the maximum dose of Cialis does not work, or your nerve damage impacts your groin area." The solutions included:

Injection Therapy:

Injection therapy requires the man to use a small needle to inject medication directly into the penis. The medicine relaxes the blood vessels and allows for increased blood flow into the penis, creating an erection. Injections are effective, fast-acting treatments because the medicine is delivered directly into the penis. The needle used is very fine, so pain from the injection site is usually minimal. It is very important that you receive these injections from a trained urologist. Penile injections not administered under the supervision of a urologist or other trained medical professional can result in serious side effects in some men.

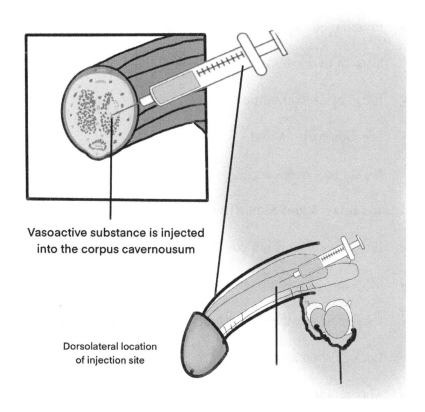

Vasoactive substance is injected
into the corpus cavernousum

Dorsolateral location
of injection site

To help maintain the erection, put a "Cockring" around the base of your penis. A "Cockrings" is a circular band that "wraps" around the base of the penis and helps maintain an erection.

They come in many different sizes and can be purchased at most "Adult Stores."

Advantages:

- Erection occurs in five to 20 minutes following injection and lasts up to one hour

- It can be used anytime

- Erection feels natural

- No surgery necessary

Disadvantages and Side Effects:

- It can be costly if not covered by insurance

- May cause bleeding and scarring at the injection site

- It can cause painful erections that last longer than two hours

- Lack of spontaneity

- May require surgery if erection is prolonged

- 75 percent of men stop using injections after one year

Vacuum Erection Device for the Treatment of ED

A plastic cylinder is placed over the penis, and a pump (either manual or battery operated) creates vacuum suction within the cylinder, drawing blood into the penis to create an erection.

A stretchable tension band placed at the base of the penis can

help maintain the erection.

Advantages:

- Economical

- It can be used anytime

  - It takes only five to ten minutes to apply

  - No side effects

  - No surgery or injections involved

Disadvantages and Side Effects:

  - May interfere with foreplay and inhibit sensuality

  - Body shape may make it difficult to use the device

  - The penis may be floppy during erection

  - May inhibit the normal flow of ejaculation

  - Lack of spontaneity

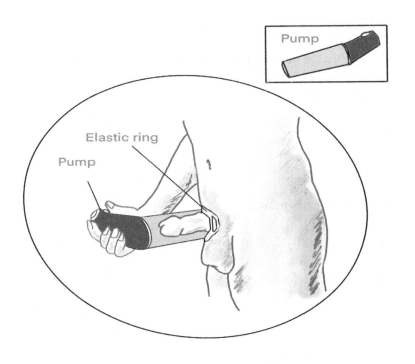

Pump

Elastic ring

Pump

Penile Prostheses (Implants) for the Treatment of ED:

Penile implants are a permanent, effective treatment for erectile

dysfunction. A penile implant is also called a penile prosthesis.

that are implanted in the penis and a pump in the scrotum that

creates an erection when the patient squeezes it. The implant in-

cludes a saline reservoir in the abdomen, which provides fluid to

create the erection. Further, research shows that penile prosthe-

ses are more satisfying than other common treatment options.

The two- and three-piece inflatable prosthetic devices consist of a fluid-filled pair of cylinders implanted in the penis and a small pump implanted in the scrotum. Both are simple to use, completely concealed inside the body, and produce an erection that looks and feels natural. With the two-piece implant, you simply squeeze and release the pump several times. When the fluid is pumped into the cylinders, it creates an erection that provides rigidity.

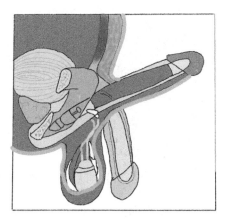

The three-piece inflatable device has an additional part – a reservoir that is implanted into the lower abdomen. When you are ready to have sex, you pump the fluid from the reservoir into the cylinders to create a rigid erection. After intercourse, you release the valve inside of the scrotum to drain the fluid back into the reservoir to return to flaccidity. The three-piece inflatable penile prosthesis creates a firmer erection than the two-piece device.

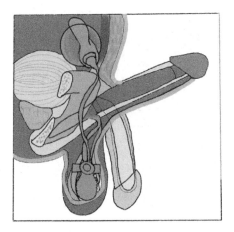

Dr. ED then pulled out a model of a "Penal Implant" and walked me through its mechanism and use.

"This is a permanent procedure, so if you decide you don't like it, there is no going back."

"Would sex stiff feel the same? Would I still ejaculate?"

"Yes, on both, Mr. Dunbar."

"So, what would you recommend?"

"I would start with the injection as it has great results. In fact, we can give you a shot now to see if it works."

"Shot now?! Sure, why not? I am open to anything!"

I just sat there with this dumb look on my face, as I thought Penal Implants were just for cosmetic reasons; now I see it was born out of a desire to correct Erectile Dysfunction.

"You have already made lifestyle changes losing 90 pounds, and I will give you a testosterone test just to be sure there are no deficiencies. Also, the best thing you can do is strengthen that lower area of your body. Have you ever considered Aquatic Therapy?"

"I am an avid swimmer but never considered Aquatic Therapy."

"Find a good Aquatic Therapist as they can help you build strength in your lower back, which would help mitigate your erectile dysfunction. Do you have any questions, Mr. Dunbar?"

"Perfect, we will be back with the "shot" for you to test...."

So that was my appointment Dr. Feelings, and it was all so surreal?

"Which part, Mr. Dunbar, finding out Dr. ED was a woman or the idea that you might need a shot in your penis or penal Implant?"

"Okay. I was caught off guard at first, but Dr. ED was extremely thorough. I "Googled' her and found she did her medical training at Temple, which is a good program, has over 30 years of experience, and is a Clinical Assistant Professor at the Emory School of Medicine."

"How did the "shot work?"

"I was expecting Dr. "ED" to come back, but then a man came into the room and stated he needed to inject the "solution" into my penis. I was shocked at first, but then I "whipped" it out as he got the shot ready for use."

I asked him if this shot was the "**Super Soldier Serum**" for the penis?"

Laughing, he said, "Naah Man, it's more like the *Incredible Hulk* as it often does a GREAT job!" So, he grabbed my privates, then stuck the needle in the right side of my Penis. I felt a pinch, then felt the fluid flow into my Penis. The nurse then told me to rub myself, and he would be back in 10 minutes to see if my erection had returned.

"What, he told you to masturbate right there?"

"Yes, Dr. Feelings! So, I did it, and *The Incredible Hulk of Erections* popped out."

I had not been that hard in YEARS!

He came back into the office and said, "Mission accomplished, you are real firm," as he grabbed my penis to ensure it was firm. This was the first time a man had ever grabbed my penis this way, and I found myself wanting Dr. ED to finish the exam.

"That is so funny, Mr. Dunbar; what happened then?"

"He told me to come back to the office IF the erection did not go down in two hours. I left the office with a "stiff dick," and I stayed erect. Nothing I did would stop the erection. I went to the bank, put air in my tires, and even fully masturbated, and I remained erect. I was so ERECT that my lower back was in pain, and still, the erection would not cease.

Finally, I went to the bathroom, and the erection stopped—the total "erection" time was about two hours from the time of the injection."

"A two-hour erection – think that will make your wife happy in the future?"

"Oh, stop, Dr. Feelings. This shot seems to be better than Cialis. Last weekend, Monique went to a Medical Conference downtown, and we rented a room for the weekend. It was a nice evening of dancing and drinking, and then when it came time to "dance," I did not show up at the party. I've already asked Dr. ED for the 20mg dosage tablets."

"Mr. Dunbar, is this your ego talking?"

"Women just don't understand how embarrassing it is that you can't take off business anymore."

"And you think Women do not feel this way?"

"Stop playing with me, Dr. Feelings. What I need is a SOLUTION, not leading questions."

"You are a finance man Mr. Dunbar. Have you done the cost-benefit of using Cialis versus Shot versus Penal Implant assuming 15 years of use?"

"No, but it would be relatively easy:

Cost Benefit Analysis	Two Months		Yearly Costs		15 Yearly Costs	
Cialis - Retail Price	$	195	$	1,170	$	17,550
Cialis - Good Rx Card	$	40	$	240	$	3,600
Incredible Hulk Shot: (10 Doses)	$	167	$	1,002	$	15,030
Penal Implant:						
Insurance Deductible = $4500	NA		NA		$	4,500

Damn! No wonder it took two months to get an appointment with Midtown Urology; if you do the math, getting the penal implant was a "no-brainer," especially if it was covered by your insurance.

"Was that "SOLUTION" good enough for you, Mr. Dunbar?

"Yes."

"Chronic Pain can be devastating to a marriage, 80% of the time leading to divorce."

"I had no idea the stats were so high. A friend of mine said she was proud of me for taking action with my physical and mental health during my pain journey. She stated her husband got hurt in a vehicle accident, suffered from chronic pain, and refused to take those affirmative steps. Why? Because of the ego and cultural norms around being "weak" for seeking mental health treatment. It cost them their marriage, as his pain produced a fit of anger that consumed their relationship."

"It's good that you know what's at stake, Mr. Dunbar, and I can't wait to see which option you select."

"Thank you, Dr. Feelings."

"I liked Dr. ED's idea about Aquatic Therapy. Have you found anyone?"

"Yes, I did! The place is located at the Beulah Missionary Baptist Church in Decatur, GA."

"Good luck Mr. Dunbar; see you next month."

Chapter 19

AQUATIC AND LAND THERAPY

"The best part of my day is swimming and exercises in warm water. Not only do I not feel pain, but at times, I feel God's loving embrace."

I am rarely on this south side of Interstate 20. Decatur is divided by I-20: The south side is uniquely African American, and the Whiteside – north side; is known for its 2-bedroom "fixer-uppers worth over $700K. I drove about five miles of the interstate and found the Beulah Missionary Baptist Church. The building was an amazing site, looking like the city of OZ as you drove closer to the chapel. They had a Wellness center in the back, and it looked like a YMCA.

I was meant by someone at the front counter, who looked at me suspiciously as if I was an unknown. Informing her of my Aquatic Therapy appointment, she directed me to the Men's room, and I could not help hearing the great music being played over the speakers. A nice blend of R&B and Jazz, perfect to settle my nerves for this new "adventure."

Aquatic Therapy refers to treatment and exercises performed in water for relaxation, fitness, physical rehabilitation, and other therapeutic benefits. I was unclear how this type of "Therapy" would work when all the hundreds of hours of physical therapy I had over the years had failed. I walked the following:

- "Old Gangsta" playing spades.
- Full basketball court.
- An impressive gym.

Every member of the church had access to these services. I then walked into the pool, and an aquatics provider took me to her office and began an extremely painful exam. They stretched and bent me to obtain a baseline; before asking if I was willing to put in the work to become healthy. I told them I would do whatever it takes to get well; she replied: Good, there will be *PAIN, PAIN, and more PAIN* before there was any gain.

Arriving early two days later, I watched as several aquatic thera-pists worked with their patients. I was informed that Vicki would be working with me and that she was located on the far side of the pool. Vicki was very attractive! She looked biracial – perhaps Afro-Latina – and I watched in awe as she caressed, coached, and guided her patient with a tenderness I had never re-ceived with a "rehab" provider in the past. My thought was sim-ple: I am really going to enjoy aquatic rehab!

"This HURTS!" I yelled as Vicki demanded I twist in the water. "You give 200% when working with me; always remember that before our sessions."

Where was the soft angelic creature, I saw the other day as she pushed my body beyond its limits? I had to say; they brought the PAIN! Finally, a rehab team that did not treat me like an 80-year-old.

"Ahhh, you in pain, *SO WHAT*! Here is how you stop the pain: Teaching me a stretch in the pool that stopped the pain; NOW, do the exercise again!"

Vicki also kept feeling my gut and stated, "We are going to work on your upper abs, your mid abs, and **REALLY ON YOUR LOWER ABS**"!!!

I felt insulted as my stomach looked much better than it did when I was 350lbs and possessed a 54-inch waist. We did things like:

- Interval Sprints.

- T-stretches.

- Dips on the corner of the pool.

- Push out of the pool.

- Lunges and Squats from the pool's latter.

I would come home in pain every day, ice my lower bag and pray for the pain to stop. Aquatic Therapy is kicking my butt. I swam in the heated pool after class the stretched to decrease the aches. Vicki really knew her stuff as I began to feel stronger as the routines became easier. Then one day, she told me to get out of the pool so she could use her cupping machine to break through my scar tissue.

Cupping has been used in the Asian world for thousands of years to treat pain. Typically, small "shots" like glass are placed on the area needing treatment in a manner that creates a vacuum. The suction created helps the blood flow in the injured area, which helps it heal. Vicki's device looked like a suction cup on the point of a gun. As she pulled the trigger, I felt the suction begin to work – yanking at the scar tissue.

I became uncomfortable as she worked my body. Still having a stomach and curves, I felt totally exposed to everyone walking around the pool as Vicki twisted/bent my body to obtain a better suction with her cupping gun. I tried to hide my discomfort, but there must have been something in my eye as Vicki looked at me and stated:

"You're in Chronic Pain. Don't you have more important things to worry about than people seeing your curves?"

I looked at her, and then a wave of contentment came over me, realizing that she was correct. It was like magic; suddenly, I became comfortable with her, with people seeing me, with being in my own skin. I was finally comfortable in my own skin, and it came because of having Chronic Pain.

Vicki would later tell me that she was a pain patient. She stated that it took five years of aquatic therapy, weight training, and lots of stretching for her to have a regular life.

"Are you still in pain?" I asked.

"Yes, I am still in pain and refuse to get a back surgery as I've worked on too many people that have unsuccessful outcomes."

That comment sent me into a tailspin as I saw aquatic therapy as the last nonsurgical hope to cure my Chronic Pain.

"Listen, Jackson; there is no cure for Chronic Pain due to scar tissue. Why? Because scar tissue grows back after it is removed, in some cases, it comes back worse."

"So why am I doing all this work, Vicki? Should I just give up? There must be a way to solve this problem?"

"There is…"

- Stretch every day for 30 minutes to an hour.

- Continue to drop weight and strengthen your core.

- Never stop swimming.

- Aquatic and Land Therapy must become staples in your exercise plan.

- Find a Message Therapist who focuses on **Deep Tissue Myofascial Release**.

Myofascial (my-o-FASH-e-ul) release is a manual therapy technique often used in massage. The technique focuses on pain believed to arise from myofascial tissues — the tough membranes that wrap, connect, and support your muscles. The focused manual pressure and stretching used in myofascial release therapy loosen up restricted movement, leading indirectly to reduced pain.

Vicki and I worked together two days a week for almost two years. She taught me that my lower "gut" acted as an anchor on my lower abs, causing more pain. The bottom line is that a strong core and smaller abs translated into better-managed pain and quality of life. So, on the days I did not see here, I would stretch and complete exercises to **stabilize/stretch** my lower back:

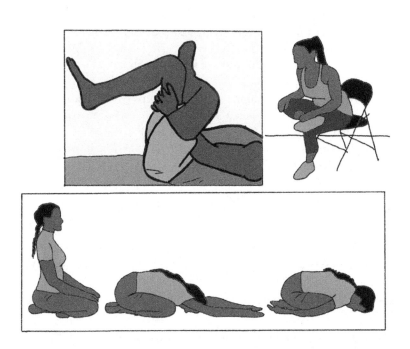

- 1: Quadriceps Stretch – Side-lying (20-sec hold – 2 sets)

- 2: Standing Calf Stretch - (20-sec hold – 2 sets)

- 3: Piriformis Stretch: Supine strong -- 10 reps (2x seconds (2x)

- 4: Seated Figure Four: (20-sec hold – 2 sets)

- 5: Child Pose: Hold for 10 seconds (2x)

- 6: Bridges: (30 reps – 2 sets)

A picture is worth 1000 words, so please find pictures of my favorite stretching exercises that I complete two to three times daily – more if it is a cold rainy day to manage pain. Copy and paste the name of these exercises on Google or YouTube for more detailed information.

For immediate pain relief, the **Cat Pose is my favorite**, as I can "knock out" a few sets when the pain gets *BAD,* then return to the matter at hand. Lastly, bridges are a good exercise as they strengthen some of the core and lower back muscles used during sex. Search the names of these exercises on Google or You-

Tube for more detailed step-by-step information.

My **Land "core" exercises** were developed by a trainer named

Dave at Pro Design Fitness, located on the first floor of the

Midtown Urology building in Midtown Atlanta. He focused on

"trunk stabilization" and a very strong "core," so my exercises

included, but were not limited to:

- Deadbugs – (20 reps – 2 sets).

- Lumbar Flexion with Rotation: Hold for 10.

- Crunches - (40 reps– 2 sets).

- Leg Raises: (2 sets of 25).

- Planks (30 sec hold – 2 sets).

- Core Ball Transfer: (25 reps, 2 sets).

- Advanced Birddog: (15 reps, 2 sets).

Stretching and Core exercises must be done every day to better manage pain. I remember a "Twilight Zone" episode where an alcoholic was forced to take a "pill" as punishment for his excessive drinking. The "pill" not only stopped his ability to get a "buzz' from drinking; it also caused him GRAVE stomach pain when he consumed alcohol. In the end, the pain was so great that he stopped drinking forever.

We are living a similar existence as Chronic Pain patients. The above stretching and core exercises help "loosen up" and strengthen core muscles which help **MANAGE** my pain. What happens if I don't do the exercises: **Pain escalates with a vengeance**, and I have a very bad day!

Any exercise to **build strength/tone** in the gym can be completed in the pool. My Strengthening/Toning **Pool** routine includes:

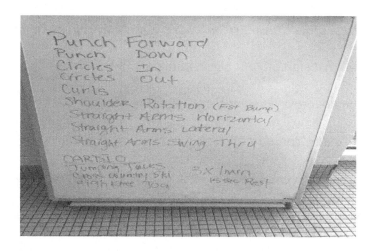

Grab two pool dumbbells and get into at least 5 feet of water and engage your core – suck in your stomach, squat a bit for a stronger stance, and remember to breathe:

- **Punch Forward**: With the two dumbbells – punch forward with the left, pull it back, then punch with the right alternating, then continue for one minute.

- **Punch Down**: Punch toward the floor of the pool, alternating right and left for a minute.

- **Circle In**: "*Chest Fly*" Imagine giving a Big Bear Hug and bringing both fists to your chest, then repeat for one minute.

- **Circle Out**: "*Reverse Chest Fly*" With both elbows slightly bent, fist start at your chest, with a dumbbell in each hand, then do a reverse Bear Hug.

- **Shoulder Rotation**: Keeping your elbows on your side around the crease of your hips, with weights in both hands, extend out, then bring them back to the center; then repeat.

- **Straight Arms Horizontal**: Extend arms out in front of you, with weights in both hands, then bring each arm down to your sides, raise arms up to the top of the water, then bring them back down to the sides; repeat.

- **Straight Arms Lateral**: Extend arms out sideways, with weights in both hands, then bring each arm down to your sides, raise arms up to the top of the water, then bring them back down to the sides; repeat.

- *Straight Arms Swing Thru*: Extend arms down with weights in both hands, then swing left arm forward and right arm back; repeat.

- *Jumping Jacks*: Start with feet together and your arms at your side; pool weights are in each hand; Jump by moving your legs outward and, at the same time, bringing your arms to the top of the water. Jump again to return to the starting position with your feet together and your arms at your side, repeat.

- *Cross Country Ski*: Extend arms down with weights in both hands, then swing left arm forward and right leg back; alternating, then swing right arm forward and left arm back; repeat.

- *High Knee Jog*: Holding weights in each hand, jog in place with knees coming off the ground.

- **All Exercises** (1) minute each, 15-second rest after each exercise, repeat for three sets.

Squats

Jumping Jacks

Jogging in place

Pushouts

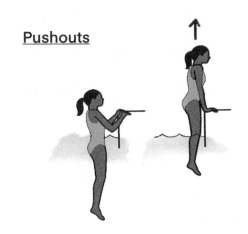

My pool cardio exercises are my favorite as I can let myself go often with minimum pain. They include:

- **Interval "Sprints"** 25 meters in less than 30 seconds, rest one minute, repeat 4x.

- **Interval** "Sprints" 25 meters in less than 30 seconds, run in place 30 seconds, rest 30 seconds, repeat 4x.

- **Squats** 25x, rest one minute, repeat 2x.

- **Jumping Jacks** 25x, rest one minute, repeat 2x.

- **Jogging in Place**: Two minutes, rest 30 seconds, repeat 2x.

- **Squat 25x**, rest 30 seconds, alternate with Jumping Jax 25x.

- **Pushouts** 20x, repeat 3x.

Other exercises include, but are not limited to:

- **Planks** on a pool noodle: Hold for 60 seconds, repeat 2x.

- **Pool Bicycles**: 25 meters, rest one minute, repeat 4x.

- **Reverse Crunches**: Holding the edge of the pool, set of 25, repeat 2x.

Combined, my EXERCISE PLAN is as follows:

- **_Mon/Friday:_**

  o Stretch: **_In the morning and before bed_**

  o Swim 800 meters

  o Land Exercises

  o Sauna/ Steam – 15 min

  o Whirlpool – 15 min

  o **_Note_**: I complete **_Land Exercises_** in the Sauna/Steam

- **_Wed:_**

  o Stretch: **_In the morning and before bed_**

  o Strength/Toning Exercises – repeat (3x)

  o Sauna/Steam – 15 min

  o Whirlpool – 15 minutes

  o **_Note_**: I complete **_Land Exercises_** in the Sauna/Steam

- **_Tues/Thurs:_**

  o Stretch: **_In the morning and before bed_**

  o Interval "Sprints" – Eight Laps

  o Pool Cardio Exercises

  o Land Exercises

- o Sauna/Steam – 15 min

- o Whirlpool – 15 min

- o *Note*: I complete *Land Exercises* in the Sauna/Steam

- **Sat:**

  - o Take a day off

- **Sun:**

  - o Stretch Exercises

  - o Land Exercises

  - o Sauna/Steam – 15 min *Note*: I complete *Land Exercises* in the Sauna/Steam

  - o Whirlpool – 15 min

It took me about a year to build up to all these routines. I would begin by showing the routines to your certified Aquatic or Land Rehab Therapists to obtain their approval. In the beginning, I could barely swim 25 meters or complete 20 partial sit-ups; but I put in the work, which strengthened my core and helped manage my back pain.

Vicki then surprised me one day....

"It's time for you to leave and concentrate on Land Therapy."

"No, there is so much more I need to learn, and you were the best Rehab provider – Water or Land – that I have ever met."

"Thank you, Jackson, but you can't live in the water your whole life. The next step for you is Land Therapy, which helps builds up your pain tolerance so you can have a more active life. Additional surgery will not help your pain, and more medication will increase your cognitive impairment. So, find a land Rehab provider that can push you towards normalcy."

I thought about Vicki's comments while driving my daughter to the pharmacy and beauty store. It was time to renew my medication, and my daughter needed more moisturizer so I could wash her hair.

Over the last five years, I've had hundreds of hours of traditional land therapy, and none of them pushed me as hard as Vicki – who works with Aquatic Fit Club. While waiting behind two

White women in the pharmacy line, I heard one woman ask questions about her Tramadol medication, and the other asked about Suboxone.

Tramadol and Suboxone are "Schedule III" drugs used for the treatment of pain but have the potential to cause abuse. Both medications are far stronger than the pain medications I am prescribed. I became enraged because these White women were able to get stronger medication for their pain relief, probably due to the Institutional Racism in pain management discussed earlier in this book. Also, I was using a scooter at the time, and both women did not. I wanted to scream! I picked up my medication, took my daughter to the Beauty Store, and the young clerk yelled, "Old Man Back Off from the Door!"

At that time, I was 6'1 and 248lbs; the clerk was 5'9 and 160lbs. He was only being rude because I was on my scooter. Already in a bad mood due to what occurred at the pharmacy, I became more enraged and yelled, "This Old Man can kick your ass, bring your Candy Ass out here so I can give you the "whipping" your daddy should have given you!"

I was tired of being on ineffective medication due to inequitable pain treatment and **More Than Tired** of society treating me like a "less than" because of the scooter. I "BANGED" on the glass door and kept yelling at this kid. Then I looked around and could not find my daughter – she had vanished!

In a panic, I put the scooter at its highest speed, looking for my daughter, who was standing by my car. "Why did you run off?" I screamed.

"I got scared, Daddy!!"

I could see it in her eyes, she was afraid of me, and that feeling cut me like a knife. Where was that levelheaded and disciplined man that kept everyone calm after the accident in 2015? Somehow, I degenerated to a point where there was little management of my emotions. Monique and I spoke about everything over dinner; she stated it might be time to add a Psychiatrist to my team.

Dr. Feelings is a Psychologist who helps people cope with life issues and mental health challenges. When you visit a Psychologist, they study the way you think, behave, and relate to other people and your environment. On the other hand, Psychiatrists are medical doctors who evaluate, diagnose, and treat people living with mental health disorders that range in severity from mild and temporary to severe and chronic."

"Our team's been looking for a Psychiatrist who can help you better manage your mental health. I think a more "pharmacological" approach to your mental health treatment can only be an enhancement to your current treatment plan."

"Do you have someone in mind, thinking how embarrassed I was for my daughter to see me in such a state?"

"I do, her name is Dr. WellMind, and she can see you in two weeks."

Chapter 20

PSYCHIATRY

"I chose to focus on the light in front of me instead of the regret that was behind."

Enjoying a cup of coffee, I waited in my home office for Dr. WellMind to log into our Video Call. Dr. Feelings and I had not spoken in weeks due to conflicting schedules, so moving forward on my mental health was top of mind. Monique stated Dr. WellMind was Emory-Trained as well and was a Forensic Psychiatrist. This meant she was a "triple threat" provider possessing certifications in Adult, Child, and Forensics Psychiatry. Suddenly, I heard, "Hello, Mr. Dunbar," and Dr. WellMind was not what I expected.

Dr. WellMind looked like one of those "Celebrity Psychiatrists" one sees on Television. Well dressed in the latest fashion, attractive, very dynamic, and extremely knowledgeable as we talked for almost three hours. She put me at ease in moments as we talked about everything that had occurred during the last five years. Her approach was somewhat different than Dr. Feeling's, focusing on my medication's effectiveness as well as reviewing my medical plan in its entirety. She asked questions about the specialties on my health plan: Pain, Primary Medicine, and Urology, and came up with one conclusion: I was undermedicated for effective pain management.

I teared up because a Medical Doctor finally believed me that my current pain medication plan was not enough.

"Not only are you undermedicated for effective pain management, but some of those medications cause irritability, depression, insomnia, and weight gain. No wonder you found it hard to manage your emotions and lose weight after your surgery. From a pharmacological point of view, your Mental Health has not been managed during the last five years, and Chronic Pain heavily impacts the mind as well as the body!

As for losing weight, Gabapentin causes weight gain. Your dosage of this medication more than tripled after the surgery, so this may be the reason why it became more difficult for you to manage your weight."

"So, how do we proceed, Dr. WellMind? I can't tell you how vindicated you made me feel. My providers seemed to ignore me every time I told them my pain was almost driving me nuts."

"How are your interactions with people currently?"

"Not good! I seemed to have zero patients for people or their bullshit, and it does not take much to lose my temper. For this reason, I've been staying home and segregating myself from everyone out of fear of exploding."

"How much do you sleep?"

"Up to five hours a day, and I feel "high" all day as my cognitive impairment seems to be at its worse."

"Do you work? How do you produce income?"

"I retired from WellMed/Atlanta, a company I started back in 2007, due to many of the issues we discussed today. I received a settlement from Snake 1 and Snake 2 in 2018. My lawyer, Peter called me and said,

"Jackson, I have good news, both Snake 1, the driver's insurance company, and Snake 2, your insurer, settled at policy limits – which meant the highest award per the insurance contracts."
Your deposition was perfect as you came off as a "Good Plaintiff." If you do the math, they awarded:

{2.5 * medical bills up to my policy limits}"

To explain properly, he gave me the following example:

So, if the driver's policy limits were $50,000 and yours were $150,000, and your medical billables were $75,000, then:

- Snake 1 pays up to $50,000 satisfying their legal obligation.

- Snake 2 pays up to $150,000 satisfying their legal obligation.

- Possible Award: Up to $200,000

- Medicals: (2.5x * 75,000) = $187,500

- **Insurance Check = $187,500** because it's under its $200,000 your insurance payout limit.

"Do you understand the example, Jackson?"

"Yes! Peter, I understood everything. Let me know when they give you an exact amount, then wire the funds into my account."

"How did that make you feel?" asked Dr. WellMind?

"It was very anticlimactic as I thought about all the money my company lost because due to my "departure." Don't get me wrong; I was happy to receive the funds as we:

- Paid off all credit debt.

- Eliminated any car loans.

- I bought my wife something nice.

- Built a three-to-six-month emergency fund.

- Invested in leading Commodity ETFs that had 20% to 30% returns and paid quarterly and yearly dividends."

"So, you got PAID?"

"I would give it all up for one pain-free day!"

"Mr. Dunbar, have you ever thought about what you gained from the surgery?"

"What I gained?!"

"Yes, think about it, you are very process-oriented:

Lost Weight:

- o Applying business concepts like S.M.A.R.T to your health, you created exercise and food plans that helped you lose almost 100lbs.

- o Further, **you never gained the weight back** even though you were on more than one medication which makes people gain weight.

Got Paid

- o You created a process for speaking with car insurance companies in a manner that leads to them paying you the maximum award under your and the driver's insurance policies.

- o As for the health insurance company, you stopped them from delaying payment of your medical bills.

- o Lastly, instead of spending all of your settlement, you invest it wisely in a manner that produces quarterly and yearly income for your family and health expenses.

You Thrived!

- o You found the experts that taught you how to reduce your pain. That costs time and a lot of money, but the pain reduction methods you acquired helped you thrive both physically and mentally during this difficult time, despite your injury.

As Dr. WellMind talked, I thought about the "Angel Clarence" from It's "A Wonderful Life" – who told George Bailey that "He had a Wonderful Life." I just sat there with a stupid look on my face – She was right!

"Mr. Dunbar, you are like an artist that is so engrossed in the details of their project that they can't take a step back and "SEE" their masterwork!" – Look at what you accomplished!! Have you ever been sick since getting in shape?"

You are right, Dr. WellMind; I've never caught so much as a sniffle since dropping all that weight!"

"Take some time and ponder that perhaps the pain has given you the gift of a longer life, sound finances, and the drive to always remain healthy."

I just sat there with a stupid look on my face, thinking of all the time spent focusing on the dark behind me and not the light ahead.

"As for your medications, I will:

- Increase your Cymbalta to better manage your pain
- Give you Seroquel to help with irritability, mood, and sleep
- Put you on Vyvanse to help with attention and weight management.

"Let me know if you have any concerns with the new medications, and I will see you in a month."

Chapter 21

ALTERNATIVE MEDICINE

"We should change the name of Alternative Medicine to "Original Medicine" because humans have used it for thousands of years. Modern/Western Medicine is only 100 years old."

It took a few days, but I finally began to sleep through the night, something I had not done in years. I was yelling less in a few weeks and felt more focused and energized for the first time in years. Monique stated that Vyvanse when given to people without ADHD, gives them energy and focus on the short term. The drug also helps with weight loss which would help my pain management.

The "degree" of focus was like nothing I've ever felt in the past. For example, I could look at a particular position in the stock market and analyze the "hell" out of it, to the point where I began to make "real' money day trading. Monique laughed and stated:

"You've had this talent the entire 20 years we've been together, and you never thought about using it?"

Vyvanse made me feel like an "Ubermensch" or Superman until it wore off; at that time, the cognitive impairment and weakness I've come to know and love over the years came back with a vengeance.

Over the next months, I timed the effectiveness of my new medications and discovered an averaged two (2) to three (3) hour window of "PEAK" effectiveness before crashing– which began an hour after taking Vyvanse. I used that time to:

- Trade the Stock Market.
- Solve any family-related issues.
- Research alternative methods to address my chronic pain.

Dr. Feelings and I had often spoken about Alternative Medicine to address my pain, but I only focused on traditional **evidence-based** Western Medicine; now, it was time to try something else.

<u>ACUPUNCTURE:</u>

I was shocked that Emory offered Acupuncture as part of their Pain Management platform. Dr. Pain-Free informed me that my sessions would be covered by insurance, which meant my out-of-pocket costs were only $60 dollars, on average, about $40 dollars less than what I found in stand-alone Acupuncture clinics and Message studios in Atlanta.

The provider was Dr. Needles, who received her master's degree in Oriental Medicine from the East-West College of Natural Medicine. I also read she was nationally board-certified, has a Diplomat of Acupuncture, and specializes in pain management, mental health, and fertility.

As I finished reading her Bio, Dr. Needles came into the office and introduced herself. She was Latina -- Cubana specifically – about 5'2 and very attractive. We talked for almost an hour as she accessed my injuries and obtained my history. She then explained the science of Acupuncture:

"Mr. Dunbar, **Acupuncture** is one of the most popular practices of Traditional Chinese Medicine in the West; it is used to prevent, diagnose, and treat disease as well as to improve general health. It is a complete medical protocol focused on correcting imbalances of energy in the body. Acupuncture is used to treat a wide variety of diseases and conditions that include but are not limited to **<u>Chronic and Acute Pain</u>**, headaches and other neurological disorders, stress and anxiety, gastrointestinal disorders, fertility, and even aesthetics."

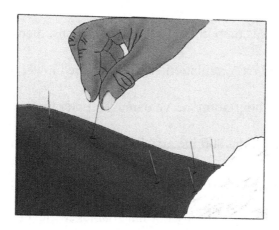

"So, are you ready for treatment?"

Soon Dr. Needles was placing needless in my lower back, down the "nerve root" of my left leg, on my forehead, and on the very top of my head. She turned off the lights and left me alone in the dark, waiting for some type of feeling. Suddenly, she opened the door saying:

"Time to wake up, Mr. Dunbar; how do you feel?"

"Is it over already?"

"You slept for about 30 minutes."

"I had no idea; everything just felt really comfortable."

"Give it a few sessions, and you will begin to feel the impact."

Dr. Needles was on point; it took three sessions, then I felt a "warmth" and/or "circulation" in the damaged lower left side of my body that housed my nerve damage. Later that day, I swam my best time of the 800 meters, was able to improve my stretching and core routines, and my mood felt good. The effects were temporary. I returned to my normal "damaged" levels the next day: A pattern that exists to this day. My sessions are twice a

month, and I wish they could occur every day.

DEEP TISSUE

Deep Tissue Myofascial Release

I had to "kiss many frogs" before finding a Massage Therapist that performed Deep Tissue Myofascial Release Massages consistently well. Massage is a broad term and can include a variety of techniques, forms, and strokes, but most people consider it to be long or short strokes and kneading with varying pressure. Myofascial release, on the other hand, is very precise and is meant to address specific areas of pain, abnormal movements, and otherwise "fix" issues you might have.

Fascia is a thin yet strong connective tissue that wraps around and intertwines literally every organ, muscle, bone, tendon, ligament, joint, and nerve, even down to the smallest of fibers within them. When the fascia surrounding a muscle becomes tense, the muscle can no longer fully function because it's being constricted by this sleeve of connective tissue.

The real difference lies in how MFR is performed so that this connective tissue is addressed. Instead of just massaging into the muscles, MFR uses slow, steady pressure along with sustained stretching to gently soften that fascia over and through the muscles, more effectively releasing the tension throughout. The provider not only works on the area of pain but rather continues working on other areas that may be the origin of the problem. As the fascia releases, the nervous system relaxes, and the muscle loosens, decreasing your pain.

It took two years, but **Shanese Marks – the owner of Well Kneaded** -- got it "right"! Located in Brookhaven, Georgia, she started around my damaged area and, thin, "bit by bit," began attacking the "fascia/scar tissue" that was causing me so much pain, and it hurt! The provider told me our sessions would get easier the longer we worked together. However, it took about two months before my "ouch ouching" stopped, and I began to look forward to the sessions.

My provider could feel a big "lump" in the area surrounding the incision point of my surgery and often joked if the surgeons left "gauze in the wound" by accident. Regardless, I soon discovered that this massage therapy became a much-needed component of my health plan, as it kept my damaged nerve areas less constricted.

Another tool used by my message therapist is Cupping: An ancient form of alternative medicine in which a therapist puts special cups on your skin for a few minutes to create suction. People get it for many purposes, including to help with pain, inflammation, blood flow, relaxation, and enhanced mobility as a type of deep-tissue massage.

The cups may be made of:

- Glass
- Bamboo
- Earthenware
- Silicone

Cupping Therapy might be trendy now, but it's not new. It dates to ancient Egyptian, Chinese, and Middle Eastern cultures. One of the oldest medical textbooks in the world, the *Ebers Papyrus*, describes how the ancient Egyptians used cupping therapy in 1,550 B.C.

My provider places the "cup" near the focus point of pain and then creates suction by moving the "cup" up and down. You can feel the "blood flow" through your pain points, causing a temporary relief of pain. I use both Acupuncture and Deep Tissue Myofascial Release Massages in tandem: On the weeks I don't do one, I complete the other, with a better quality of life being my goal.

THE AMERICAN CANE SELF DEFENSE SYSTEM

"Disability becomes Advantage."

One night, my wife and I were going to our car after a "date night" at a local restaurant when a man surprised us by asking for money. Before I could move my scooter closer to speak with the man, my wife jumped in front of me and told the man we would buy him dinner. I was shocked! I'd studied martial arts for years – Boxing (5 years) and Muay Thai (9 Years); this fact made my wife feel safe whenever we were together. During the drive home, Monique apologized for "stepping in" and hoped I was not "hurt" by her actions. I was deeply troubled but kept that to myself as I processed that Monique might not feel safe with me anymore?

The next day, I came across an article that disabled people are disproportionately victims of violent crime and victimization in the United States; furthermore, the frequency of these crimes is also increasing. The data shows that from 2017-to 2019, disabled people accounted for 26% of nonfatal violent crimes, even though they make up only 12% of the population and are victims of violence at almost **four times the rate of non-disabled people**.

These statistics were alarming, thinking of my current medical condition: Confined to a scooter about 75% of the time, very limited mobility, needing the use of two canes to barely walk. How do I protect my family in this condition, as all my prior training required profound use of my lower body – which now caused abject pain. I then looked for a "Martial Arts Systems" for people that were disabled. I found two places in Atlanta that taught "Kali," a stick fighting system originating from the Philippines. I went to both schools and was turned down flat – as they stared at my scooter. It took several weeks, but I found an online program called the **American Cane Self Defense System, "ACSD."**

Cuban American, GrandMaster Joe Robaina created "**ACSD**" as an enhanced derivative of **Cane Do Kai**: ___Way of the Cane!___ GrandMaster Robaina's involvement in martial arts spans three decades, earning Master's ranks in Jujutsu, Aikijujutsu, Aikido, and Hapkido. He also held black belts in Judo, Taekwondo, and Isshinryu Karate and was the only 10th-degree CaneMaster certified under GrandMaster Mark Shuey.

"ACSD" is different than CDK because it teaches the "Cane" and "Open Hand" with a tactical focus; thus, ACSD is best described as the "*__Way of the Tactical Cane!__*" American Cane Martial Arts have been influenced by oriental, Filipino, and other martial methods; however, it contains characteristics that are purely American. For example, the American canes are designed with self-defense in mind against multiple knife attacks. They are made of hardwoods and/or other materials to withstand hard impact. They feature deep grooves for gouging, raking, etc., for close-range defense. The self-defense applications reflect these details.

I informed Grand Master Robaina of my injuries, and he stated the best way to begin "ACSD" is to start "*__where the student is,__*"; which means – Do what I can until my body is stronger to do more. My first class was a 'video session' with students from around the world. Most were over 60; some were disabled like me; one person was even missing a leg. As we began the lesson,

Grand Master Robaina insisted on "pinpoint" precision, as that was the only way to ensure successful "self-defense'. He stated: "I understand that many of you have "shoulder, knee, or back issues": **_SO, WHAT: The Criminals Don't Care!_** "We called the phrase a "**Joeism.**" I smiled because he reminded me of "Burgess Meredith's" character "Mickey" in the Rocky franchise. To those of us on scooters, he stated we needed the ability to "get up and down" from our seats and to move four steps left to right and back to front. GrandMaster Robaina suggested that we all perform squatting drills from our scooters to build strength.

I did those "Damn squatting drills every day, and it HURT! For example, I added five sets of squatting to my exercise routine. When the pain started, I placed a bag of "frozen peas" on my back to calm the nerves, stretched the muscles, then went back to squatting. It took months, but soon I acquired the ability to:

- Move-in a small circle around my scooter.
- Walk back and forth, side to side, on a limited basis.
- Use two canes effectively for self-defense.

Due to the permanent nerve damage in the lower left side of my body, I needed the use of two canes when practicing ACSD. It took almost a year, but my *Disability became an Advantage* as I not only became adept at two canes self-defense; but acquired more mobility on the left side of my body. As I would swing my canes from "coast to coast," I could feel my scar tissue "ripping" to make me a bit more mobile.

I never liked doing "Katas or Forms" in Martial Arts as I found it repetitive and boring. Now, perfecting my "Forms" helped me manage my Anger: I could once again "**AngerFocus**" to achieve a S.M.A.R.T goal, in part, due to ***Professor Pain***:

What is Professor Pain?

Prof. Pain is the training "dummy" that I use to practice my Ka-

tas. Suffering from depression and anxiety caused by my medi-

cation and pain; I would angrily "strike" Prof. Pain with all my

strength. In doing so, I would hurt myself, fall **or** my cane

would bounce back and hit me in the head. I had to calm down,

breathe, then focus to practice my Katas correctly, which seemed to negate any of my negative thoughts. The GrandMaster called it "Brain Balance."

"Your mind was too busy mastering the "Forms" and trying not to hit yourself with the cane to be concerned with being depressed."

"ACSD" has become a valued "tool" in my arsenal to improve my quality of life and has changed my exercise plan in the following way:

MY CURRENT EXERCISE PLAN is as follows:

- ***Mon/Friday:***
    - o Stretch: ***In the morning and before bed***
    - o Swim 800 meters
    - o Land Exercises
    - o Sauna/ Steam – 15 min
    - o Whirlpool – 15 min
    - o ***Note***: I complete ***Land Exercises*** in the Sauna/Steam
- ***Wed:***
    - o Stretch: ***In the morning and before bed***
    - o Strength/Toning Exercises – repeat (3x)

- o Sauna/Steam – 15 min

- o Whirlpool – 15 minutes

- o *Note*: I complete *Land Exercises* in the Sauna/Steam

- *Tues/Thurs:*

  - o Stretch: *In the morning and before bed*

  - o ACSD: Forms (1-4) – repeat (2x)

  - o Land Exercises

  - o Sauna/Steam – 15 min

  - o Whirlpool – 15 min

  - o *Note*: I complete *Land Exercises* in the Sauna/Steam

- Sat:

  - o OFF

- Sun:

  - o Stretch Exercises

  - o Land Exercises

  - o Whirlpool – 25 min

Like swimming, I am taken to a place that improves my mental health and strengthens my body while teaching self-defense.

ACSD is the "Land Rehab" Vicki told me to find, and it's a **non-Western** way to improve the body ***without*** additional medication or surgery. I also have a new "Cane Name" fitting my "double cane style of self-defense – ***"Big Daddy Cane;"*** for some reason, the name makes my wife laugh!

MEDICAL MARIJUANA

I found it hard to approach my providers about the use of Medical Marijuana. First, I had to deal with negative and incorrect stereotypes surrounding African Americans and the misuse of pain medications. Then I had to educate some providers about the "health" benefits of cannabis when 50% of (PCPs) feel it's not a legitimate therapy.

Luckily, in February 2019, the World Health Organization (WHO) proposed "rescheduling cannabis within international law to take account of the growing evidence for medical applications of the drug, reversing its position held for the past 60 years that cannabis should not be used in legitimate medical practice.

The first step is to become familiar with some of the evidence for using medical cannabis for pain management, particularly which types of pain appear to respond better to the substance. Also, develop a basic knowledge of the key components of cannabis (e.g., THC and CBD) and how they may affect the body, as well as available forms in which medical marijuana, cannabis, and hemp (which is a different plant and contains 0 to 3% THC) may be available for pain management.

Given the current concerns about overprescribing opioids and efforts at all levels to reduce the number of individuals who may misuse, abuse, or overdose on these drugs,[1] clinician and patients are looking for other treatment options when it comes to managing chronic pain and related symptoms.

In February 2019, the World Health Organization (WHO) proposed "rescheduling cannabis within international law to take account of the growing evidence for medical applications of the drug, reversing its position held for the past 60 years that cannabis should not be used in legitimate medical practice. https://www.practicalpainmanagement.com/patient/treatments/marijuana-cannabis/navigating-cannabis-options-pain-related-symptoms

Keeping it real, I have not found the proper "dosage" of medical marijuana that can manage my pain without causing cognitive impairment. My experimentation with Cannabis creates a feeling of "calm that starts in my head, then runs down the damaged nerve root of my body until I feel no pain. That feeling of "no pain" is euphoric but short-lived as it dissipates in roughly an hour. Technological advances in medical marijuana continue to proceed forward, and it is my hope that an alternative to Western medication is within our grasp.

Chapter 22

CONCLUSION

"Fortune favors the Bold! In other words, the ability to take risks is a necessary element to fully enjoying life at its best – I will have no regrets on my deathbed!"

"Honey, you have not touched a thing on your plate. You seem distracted, Jackson?"

"I am, Monique. Something weird happened at Becky's school today."

"Well, just don't sit there, tell me."

"Becky told me that the air conditioning went out at her school about two days ago and that her classroom gets really hot. So, I did what any father would do: I went to the local hardware store and bought all the fans. I then drove them to the school and begged the Principal to accept them as a gift."

"Begged, she was not thrilled about what you did?!"

"No, I think she felt embarrassed. I told her my goal was to cool down the classroom, that I was a father just trying to protect his girl. She then told me to get one of the janitors to help me since I was on my scooter. The custodian came and told me that he was too busy to help and that I would have to put the fans together myself."

"Really, what a jerk; how did you manage that with your pain?" "I loaded up the fans on my scooter, drove them down to the classroom, and Becky had this big smile that I brought the fans. That smile gave me the incentive to get out of the scooter, get on the floors, and starts putting together the fans. At first, the pain was incredible; but as I watched the kids and saw their happy faces as each fan was completed, then all of a sudden, I was not in pain anymore. It was weird; the more I focused on the kids and trying to make things better, the less I thought about my pain."

"What you were doing, Jackson was called *Service Leadership*: When a person *discovers their heart to serve, answers their call to lead, and summons their courage to engage*. You saw a need in the community, summoned the courage, took action, and then you made things better. I am very proud of you. Have you ever heard the motto: The best way to forget about your troubles is to help someone else?"

"Of course, but I never dreamed that "Service Leadership" could help me temporarily forget my pain. I put together each fan, the sweat just rolling down my face on that hot summer day. I then wondered what would happen if this inner-city Public School had the same parental involvement that we saw in the Private Schools?"

"Are you regretting that we pulled our kids out of Private School?"

"NO! For too many years, African Americans have had to choose between underfunded community public schools with low test scores and poor results or private schools with high test scores, but *Black and Brown* kids were treated poorly due to In-stitutional Racism. What would happen if people like us invested just 20% of that "private school money" into our local public schools – can you imagine what that would do to these schools?"

"Baby, I refuse to give another $40k a year to a private school whose **racists practices** harm the Mental Health of our children. Besides, the S.T.E.M and I.B programs of the Tucker Public Schools are free, quite competitive to be accepted, have small classroom sizes, and possess well-trained teachers dedicated to "Diversity Excellence!"

I read this article about Michael J. Fox. Apparently, he indulged in years of drinking after obtaining his Parkinson's diagnosis. Then one day, he decided to use his social capital to make the world a better place. All that to say, maybe this Chronic Strength journey that I've been on for the last five years has a purpose?

"And what would that be, hun?"

"It was creating a foundation that teaches "Revenue Literacy ©" to children, teens, and young adults."

"Are you talking about "Financial Literacy?"

"No, there is a difference: Financial Literacy teaches students to manage the money they possess; Revenue Literacy teaches students to take an idea and transform it into a product or service so they can make money. We then teach them to wisely invest in the stock market, so they can take those proceeds and create more businesses that sustain their communities."

"I love this idea, Jackson, and you have not been this excited in years, but there seems to be something on your mind?"

"There is something I must do before moving forward."

"What is it, Jack?"

"I want to attend my 20th Year Law School Reunion in New Orleans, and I want to do that by myself."

"No way! NO! Absolutely Not! You can barely get around the block, let alone in a city like New Orleans."

"Baby, I need you to calm down and listen! I lived abroad for years before we met and traveled through almost 40 different countries. There was a" **SWAG**" I used to have, which was developed from years of meeting new people in different environments, often not speaking my own language. Anyway, I lost that SWAG during the last five years, and I want it back! The only way for that to occur is for me to make this trip – Alone!"

Monique just looked me up and down, rolling her eyes as if I was about to get "cussed" out, and then said, "Well, I have work, and the kids are still in school, so it would be hard for the whole family to attend -- so what's your plan?"

"Simple, I am a disabled man, in a scooter, with plenty of credit cards to solve whatever problems life throws at me during the trip."

"Since there is no changing your mind, when do you leave?"

"In three weeks."

Hartsfield-Jackson Airport they say it's the busiest airport on the planet. I was lucky enough to find a handicapped parking spot. Luggage fits on my scooter; this should be simple, drive up to the gate and ......

I made it to the base of the escalators in the terminal to discover

they were not working. I then saw signs pointing to elevators,

but when I arrived, they had been moved as well. I could see

there was a lot of construction taking place at the airport, but it

seemed as if little thought was given to mobility services. I just

sat there in the parking lot, watching the crowds of people, hop-

ing to find a "pattern" that would direct me to the correct termi-

nal.

Ten minutes later, I was able to find an elevator that worked on

the opposite side of the parking lot. I went to the "reservations floor" and "scooted" by at least 30 people in wheelchairs waiting to be assisted by porters to their terminals. The problem is that I only see two ports available to assist all those people. "Thank God" for my scooter. I get to TSA, who sends me to the disability "fast track" line, where I find a "long line of "wheelchairs' and only one TSA agent checking our credentials. This was a serious "bottleneck" as we would require additional time due to our lack of mobility. There were three TSA agents helping those with no mobility issues, and that line moved with surprising efficiency.

I finally get through TSA, make it to my flight and discover the bag containing my medications is missing. "SHIT: I left that carry-on with TSA and only had ten minutes to retrieve it before boarding. Luckily, a TSA agent came running toward me with my bag in hand; it was my first lucky break on this trip, and hopefully, it would not be my last.

I finally made it to New Orleans. These two big creoles "Brothas" brought me my scooter and tipped them well on my way to the Airport Shuttle. The ride to the city brought back so many memories of my time in "New La." The roads were still "bumpy; we drove past my old apartment on the 3000 block of St. Charles Ave. – I used to rent my "spot" out for thousands "during Mardi gras; that Jimmy Johns is new; otherwise, downtown looks the same as we arrive at the Intercontinental Hotel which is beautiful. I called home, updated everyone on my trip, then went to sleep.

The next morning, staring into a mirror, "I look like a million dollars: New custom suit, manicured brows, and fresh hair cut lined to perfection. The scooter just throws the whole thing off; taking a deep breath, I call a cab that brings me to Weinmann Hall: The building that houses Tulane University School of Law.

My hands begin to sweat as the cab dropped me off, and a tidal wave of memories hits me while "scooting" the hallowed halls. There were easily hundreds of people walking around me, all passing out their cards and looking like they stepped off Ebony Magazine. The Tulane Alums were renowned Corporate and Criminal Lawyers, Members of Congress, and Titans of Industry. I even bumped into my old mentor Professor Rhinestone, a brilliant attorney and Statesman.

It was then that the stares began as people walked by me in their attempt to work the room. I felt nothing but anxiety, remembering my ability to "work" in a crowded room. I was great at it! It could work with the best, and now, I am running into the bathroom with my tail between my legs.

Wiping the sweat from my face, I stared into the mirror, thinking it might be time to go back home! I wondered if this was how Moses felt after 40 years in the desert: So, beaten down by life that this once would be "Pharoah" could barely speak. I pray and begin to think about everything I accomplished during the last

five years while being in constant pain. I figured out how to

make money, lose 90lbs and thrive while dealing with an injury

that made me permanently disabled. I have **CHRONIC**

STRENGTH and will be the man I used to be! Be the Black

Professor X. Speak with the same conviction on Malcolm X! Be

the combination of the two: Be Professor Malcolm X!

I came out of the bathroom filled with newfound energy while working the "room" of the conference. In fact, I used the chair to my advantage to take the power space and the power seat at the table as the conferences continued throughout the day. Then the topic turned to racism in hiring and promotion practices in Law Firms. The stories were horrid as each speaker gave details about their negative experiences during their legal careers. Some of them felt like they had no hope; it was then that the spirit took me, and I rolled my scooter to the middle of the floor:

"Hello, my name is Jackson Dunbar, Esq. I am truly humbled by the individuals in this room and ask for several minutes to speak. Many of us have faced institutional racism our entire lives and developed methods to circumvent them, as evident by your participation at this conference. The stories that I've heard today regarding racism in the workplace have been horrid, but I know there is another path: **The way of the Entrepreneur!**

Institutional Racism has always been the catalyst for the Black Entrepreneur: A tradition that goes back over 400 years to when the first Africans were brought to this continent. Even then, Black Freedmen found that there were no jobs in this "land of milk and honey." Like you, these Black Men and Women despaired, then they turned their skillsets into the first Black-Owned Businesses in this land.

You may ask, where did these Freedmen acquire these marketable skills? **From two places**:

- ***Slaves brought from Africa*** were sought due to their Agricultural expertise – stated another way, they were skilled laborers that made their so-called "masters" rich, and once freed, were able to build a legacy for themselves. As over 90% of all plantations were managed by "Slave Labor," they also had the managerial talent needed to make a success out of their businesses.

- *Free African Men and Women* who settled this land were experienced Entrepreneurs in their homeland, as evident by their trading organizations, secret societies, and merchant guilds. Those marketable skills were exported with them to this "so-called" New World, which they used to create sustaining Black-Owned Businesses despite the insidious racial practices that prevented them from full access to fair opportunities.

Like many of us here, our ancestors cultivated their entrepreneurial skills "working" for the "MAN" or acquired these marketable skills by running successful businesses. Our ancestors took their profits, built thriving communities, then repeated the process, inevitably leading to the modern African American Entrepreneur: We can do the same!

I am the Great Grandson of Jackson Dunbar: Owner of the Dunbar Hotel -- at one time, the largest Black-Owned Hotel in the state of Florida. The building is now a designated historical monument. I followed my great grandfather's example:

- I worked for the "MAN," learning all aspects of business and legal craftsmanship.

- I saved and invested my money wisely so that I would have startup capital for my own business, just in case the "bank" turned me down for a loan.

- Then created a business whose social footprint positively impacted my local community.

Yes, there were "hiccups along the way, like being rendered permanently disabled; that slowed me down a "bit," but I never gave up. If our ancestors, did it and I was able to do it, then everyone in this room can do it!

Remember, **Institutional Racism** created the Black Entrepreneur. Use your anger as a source of strength. Focus your anger on S.M.A.R.T goals to start your own businesses, then put those profits into your local community to ensure it thrives. Entrepreneurship is in our blood; all you need is just the courage to dig! Thank you!"

I received a standing ovation while scooting back to my table. My speech was unplanned and came from my heart. For the first time in five years, I felt like my old self.

Later that evening, I met Professor Rhinestone at the InterContinental Hotel for drinks.

"I know we did not have time to speak today, Professor Rhinestone, but I am glad you could come out for drinks."

"I don't get out much, Jackson, so thanks for the invitation. By the way, that was an impressive speech you gave today."

"Thank you, Professor Rhinestone. Ever since the accident, I felt like a shadow of myself, but today, it was like the spirit touched me, and I became more than my disability. Maybe, I still have something to contribute to society despite the "curve" that was thrown my way."

"Have you ever thought about public speaking or even writing a book?"

"No, besides, who would want to listen to me? I am not a rapper; I never played professional sports, and I am not a public figure like a TV star or YouTuber -- who would listen to me?"

"Don't sell yourself short, Jackson. There were judges, congressmen, business leaders, and some pretty accomplished attorneys in that room today, and you had them all wondering: Who the hell is this man, and how do I get to know him?"

"Really!"

"Yes, while you were up front, I sat in the back and watched everyone remain silent as you spoke. They were captivated by every word. You were something more! Laughing -- You could have talked for another five minutes or 50 minutes; even the keynote speaker was upset because they had to speak after you."

"I am sorry for the interruption, but the lady over there wanted you to have this glass of Champaign."

"I guess you still have it, Professor Rhinestone."

"No, sir, the drink is for you."

"Excuse me!" I looked across the bar and saw a very attractive Black Woman, 5'9, a "dark and lovely", in a tight red dress tailored made for her ass, ready for a night on the town."

"Uhm, I guess that is my cue to leave Jackson, but think about what I said, and give me a call of you to make a decision."

"I sat there like an idiot, not knowing what to do. I used to be much better at this sort of thing, but two years of marriage, two kids, a dog, and this scooter have certainly thrown a" wrench" in my "game."

"I see your friend has left; the woman stated as she came to the table. I enjoyed your speech today."

"Thank you, forgive me; I don't remember seeing you there?"

"I was sitting at one of the back tables, but I listen to every word and your eyes?"

"What about them?"

"They looked innocent, tired, hard, empathetic, and completely honest. See, so many of us are used to listening to "bullshit" all day; hearing words like yours is like eating a "snow cone" in the desert. May I join you?"

"Yes, please. Thank you for the drink and the kind words; I am Jackson."

"My name is Adele; please to meet you, Jackson Dunbar Esq, so since you piqued my curiosity, tell me your tale."

"So, you know my last name too?"

"Smiling. Yes, you lead with that at the beginning of your speech."

"Tell me your "tale," I guess you were an English major in college – laughing. Well, I am married, two kids from Atlanta, and of course, you see the obvious?"

"By that, do you mean the scooter?"

"Yes!"

"Something told me that you did not know just how attractive you really are."

I turned red, forgetting how bold some women could be, not knowing what to say...

"Jackson, no one in that room noticed your scooter. They saw a man possessed with conviction. Someone hit by life but possessing the -- what did you call it -- **Chronic Strength** to improve himself and his community.

"Guess I never looked at it that way. Thank you so much; it has been a journey. Do you come to this bar often?"

"I had a date, but the guy stood me up; that was my good luck as I found you here with your friend."

"Oh, as I said, I am married, and even if I wasn't, you would not have had a good "nightcap" with me."

"Nightcap? Guess I wasn't the only one that used to watch "Flavor of Love." By the way, is that your way of telling me your "Dick" does not work?"

Gulping down my drink and was embarrassed as hell -- but there was no way I would let Adele know that – "Yes, the plumbing does not work, and I am still waiting for my Urologists to figure out the right treatment plan".

We sat there, silent, just looking into each other's eyes, then I said, "I traveled extensively through Europe in my 20s and 30s. My favorite memory was meeting new people and sharing stories by a campfire, drinking whatever was available. That being said, I would love your company just to talk, like two strangers on a train going to a foreign destination. We probably won't see each other again, so the conversation might be enjoyable.

"Ok, Jackson, let's talk. The idea that a man's only agenda in a bar is to listen to me instead of getting into my pants is quite pleasing and very sexy."

"I am a Bourbon man; how about you?"

"I can do that dance?"

"Waiter, a bottle of Uncle Nearest if you have it, and don't disturb us the rest of the evening. We talked for hours. I learned that Adele was divorced, had one daughter, and practiced Employment Law. She was also five years younger than me and was rocking that red dress that seemed to be tailored made for her ass."

I told her everything – from the accident to the present day. She seemed happy to listen, almost as if this was the first time a man was being honest with her. Then Adele dropped a bombshell: "I know loss, not Chronic Pain, but I lost my son a few years ago to cancer, and that loss still cuts me to my core."

I could see Adele teared up as she began to speak about her son Marshall and the dreams she had for him. That loss destroyed her marriage, and Adele has never been the same since.

"What do you do to fight your depression?" I asked.

Now it was her time to be silent.

"Listen, we are both survivors of loss; the question is, how do we thrive despite that loss? One thing I can tell you, only another person going through a loss it's going to understand the pain you feel."

"So, what should I do now? How did you get to this point?"

"I won't lie to you; there will be Pain, Pain, and Pain before there is any Gain. If you are ready to do the work: It starts with building a "Thrive-Team" of Wellness who wants, you to succeed.

I became so angry when my back surgery failed, and my injuries became permanent. I was broken in body, mind, and spirit, so it became impossible to **AngerFocus**: To focus my anger in productive ways. I sought experts and methods that would improve my quality of life:

- *__Body__*: Pain Management, Primary Care, Aquatic and Land Therapy, Urology, Alternative Medicine. These providers:

    - Identified that my body was not healthy

    - It helped me formulate a plan to become healthy

    - It gave me methods to attack my pain while staying in shape

- *__Mind__*: Psychiatry, Psychology, Alternative Medicine. These providers:

    - It helped me embrace my new normal.

- It gave me methods to attach my depression and anger in positive ways.
- Supported my continued efforts of inventive self-help.

- *Spirit*: Family, God, Aquatic Therapy and ACSD
  - Assisted me during my darkest days.
  - It aided me when I became discouraged.
  - Gave me the strength to never give up.

Once I became healthy in Body, Mind, and Spirit, I was able to **AngerFocus**: To Channel my anger into S.M.A.R.T goals that make the world a better place. By doing this type of Service Leadership, I was able to thrive because life became less about my pain and more about helping others less fortunate than me. Do you understand, Adele?"

"Yes, thank you, Jackson! I am just so angry about my son being taken away."

"And you know what, that is cool. You have a right to be angry about the loss you have sustained, and anyone telling you different is full of shit! Jesus, now I am sounding like my parents.

"They must have been good people as you are a caring man."

"Thank you, Adele. I see kindness, warmth, and the heart of a warrior in your eyes. Listen, it is tough to manage anger when you've had a permanent loss. A "**Circle of WellNess**" that sustains your mind, body, and spirit not only helped me **AngerFocus**, but it showed me how to thrive despite my limitations."

After a while, I realized how late it was. "Oh crap, it's 6 am, and I have a plane to catch."

"It was a pleasure speaking with you, Jackson. I haven't had a conversation like that in years."

"You're welcome! I feel the same way and hope we were able to help each other tonight."

"So, what's next for you, Jackson?"

"I have a few ideas about how to do some good in the world, but only have a few hours a day to make them happen."

"Is that because of your limitations?"

"Yes, please say a prayer for me."

"Of course, I will, but I am curious, how are you going to accomplish your goals in only a few hours a day?"

"Oh, it is easy, Adele – I just have to be **_S.M.A.R.T_**!

BEFORE AND AFTER

Me @ 350lbs Waist 54"

Me @ 245lbs Waist "42"

JACKSON DUNBAR, ESQ.

References:

https://www.mayoclinic.org/diseases-conditions/back-pain/expert-answers/myofascial-release/faq-20058136

https://www.hr.emory.edu/NewsYouCanUse/TEC-3192%20Acupuncture%20Flyer%20v6.p

https://abcnews.go.com/US/crime-disabled-people-rising-advocates/story?id=81210410.
https://wsimag.com/science-and-technology/51588-the-art-of-cupping-therapy
https://americancaneselfdefense.com
https://americancaneselfdefense.com
https://www.coloradouro.com/conditions/erectile-dysfunction-ed/treatments-for-erectile-dysfunction/penile-prostheses-erectile-dysfunction-treatment/

https://seekingalpha.com/article/4435888-what-is-an-etf?external=true&gclid=EAIaIQobChMIkI774N-09gIVBmxvBB3WVwegEAAYBCAAEgK2svD_BwE&utm_campaign=14049528666&utm_medium=cpc&utm_source=google&utm_term=132628631894%5Eaud-1457157705279%3Adsa-1635534204689%5E%5E584965509579%5E%5E%5Eg

https://seekingalpha.com/article/4435888-what-is-an-etf?external=true&gclid=EAIaIQobChMIkI774N-09gIVBmxvBB3WVwegEAAYBCAAEgK2svD_BwE&utm_campaign=14049528666&utm_medium=cpc&utm_source=google&utm_term=132628631894%5Eaud-1457157705279%3Adsa-1635534204689%5E%5E584965509579%5E%5E%5Eg

https://www.nbcnews.com/health/kids-health/black-kids-get-less-pain-medication-white-kids-er-n427056

https://thehill.com/opinion/healthcare/583332-the-opioid-crackdown-leaves-chronic-pain-patients-in-limbo

(Politico 2018/08/28)

https://www.kff.org/other/state-indicator/opioid-overdose-deaths-by-raceethnicity/?currentTimeframe=0&sortModel=%7B%22colId%22:%22Location%22,%22sort%22:%22asc%22%7D

https://www.nbcnews.com/health/kids-health/black-kids-get-less-pain-medication-white-kids-er-n427056

https://thehill.com/opinion/healthcare/583332-the-opioid-crackdown-leaves-chronic-pain-patients-in-limbo

https://www.cdc.gov/mmwr/volumes/65/rr/rr6501e1.htm

https://thehill.com/opinion/healthcare/583332-the-opioid-crackdown-leaves-chronic-pain-patients-in-limbo

https://www.medicalnewstoday.com/articles/90-us-primary-care-offers-lower-pain-relief-doses-black-patients

https://www.hopkinsmedicine.org/opioids/what-are-opioids.html

https://www.hopkinsmedicine.org/opioids/what-are-opioids.html

https://www.kff.org/other/state-indicator/opioid-overdose-deaths-by-raceethnicity/?currentTimeframe=0&sortModel=%7B%22colId%22:%22Location%22,%22sort%22:%22asc%22%7D

https://www.politico.com/story/2018/08/28/how-the-opioid-crackdown-is-backfiring-752183

https://www.politico.com/story/2018/08/28/how-the-opioid-crackdown-is-backfiring-752183

https://www.kff.org/other/state-indicator/opioid-overdose-deaths-by-raceethnicity/?currentTimeframe=0&sortModel=%7B%22colId%22:%22Location%22,%22sort%22:%22asc%22%7D

https://www.aclu.org/other/race-war-drugs

https://www.aclu.org/other/race-war-drugs

https://www.aclu.org/other/race-war-drugs

https://www.kff.org/other/state-indicator/opioid-overdose-deaths-by-raceethnicity/?currentTimeframe=0&sortModel=%7B%22colId%22:%22Location%22,%22sort%22:%22asc%22%7D

https://www.aamc.org/news-insights/how-we-fail-black-patients-pain

https://www.pnas.org/content/113/16/4296

https://www.today.com/health/implicit-bias-medicine-how-it-hurts-black-women-t187866

https://www.washingtonpost.com/health/is-bias-keeping-female-minority-patients-from-getting-proper-care-for-their-pain/2019/07/26/9d1b3a78-a810-11e9-9214-246e594de5d5_story.html

https://www.today.com/health/implicit-bias-medicine-how-it-hurts-black-women-t187866

https://www.medicalnewstoday.com/articles/90-us-primary-care-offers-lower-pain-relief-doses-black-patients https://abcnews.go.com/Health/Wellness/black-children-pain-meds-er/story?id=16231146

Made in United States
Orlando, FL
23 June 2022

19054495R00157